Biographical Sources:

A Guide to Dictionaries and Reference Works

Biographical Sources:

A Guide to Dictionaries and Reference Works

by Diane J. Cimbala,
Jennifer Cargill, and Brian Alley

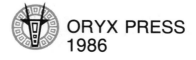
ORYX PRESS
1986

The rare Arabian Oryx is believed to have inspired the myth of the unicorn. This desert antelope became virtually extinct in the early 1960s. At that time several groups of international conservationists arranged to have 9 animals sent to the Phoenix Zoo to be the nucleus of a captive breeding herd. Today the Oryx population is over 400, and herds have been returned to reserves in Israel, Jordan, and Oman.

Copyright © 1986 by Alley, Cargill and Company and Diane J. Cimbala

Published by The Oryx Press
2214 North Central at Encanto
Phoenix, AZ 85004-1483

Published simultaneously in Canada

Printed and Bound in the United States of America

∞ The paper used in this publication meets the minimum requirements of American National Standard for Information Science—Permanence of Paper for Printed Library Materials, ANSI Z39.48, 1984.

Library of Congress Cataloging-in-Publication Data

Cimbala, Diane J.
  Biographical sources.

  Includes index.
    1. Biography—Bibliography.   2. Biography—Dictionaries—Bibliography.   I. Cargill, Jennifer S.
II. Alley, Brian.   III. Title.
Z5301.C58   1986   [CT104]   016.92   86-12805
ISBN 0-89774-136-6

Table of Contents

Acknowledgements

We would like to thank the staffs of the numerous libraries we have used both in person and via interlibrary loan, in particular Elise Little, Interlibrary Loan, Augusta College, Augusta, Georgia. Our compilation would have been much more difficult if we had not been able to take advantage of the miracles of electronic mail, online catalogs, and the many other modern library services and technologies.

We also wish to express our special thanks to our friends at Oryx Press, including our editor, Jan Krygier; vice president, editorial, Susan Slesinger; and the president of Oryx Press, Phyllis B. Steckler, whose encouragement and support are warmly appreciated.

A special thanks to Paul Cimbala for his encouragement of this project from the historian's point of view.

Introduction

Even people who dislike history cannot help but be drawn to the human part of the past. One way to study the past is through biographies of the key players in a given historical period or event. Some biographies are monographic studies of individuals while other, briefer biographies appear in one of the most basic of library reference sources: the biographical dictionary.

Biographical dictionaries are used frequently by all of us, regardless of our interests. Historians, literary scholars, and genealogists put these sources to the greatest use, but students of the "hard" and social sciences, the arts, and technology often need information about the people who have shaped and contributed to the study of their disciplines.

There is an astonishing number of biographical sources available, ranging from children's books about Revolutionary War heroes to the venerable *Dictionary of National Biography*.[1] While Eugene Sheehy's *Guide to Reference Books*[2] refers to a selection of these titles and the Gale *Biographical Index Series*[3] lists a hefty number of the more common biographical works, annotated access to most biographical dictionaries is nonexistent. We compiled *Biographical Sources: A Guide to Dictionaries and Reference Works* because we perceived a real need for annotated bibliographic access to these sources and because we have a special fondness for biography. Our intent in producing this work is to assist researchers in identifying which sources are most likely to contain personal data about the persons they are interested in studying. In addition to annotating the scope of each source, we have tried to indicate which sources contain finding aids that will assist the researcher.

Because the number of biographical sources is so overwhelming, we quickly determined that limits would have to be introduced to our title selection process. Therefore, we have excluded non-English-language materials and have emphasized those titles published or distributed in the United States and Canada. Consequently, the titles listed here have an Anglo-American bias, but then so do the reference collections of most college, university, and public libraries in the United States and Canada.

For this first edition, we declared December 31, 1984, to be the usual publication cutoff date. Future editions will include later imprints as well as titles omitted from this first effort.

Titles containing fewer than 15–20 biographical sketches were scrutinized carefully before being added to the list of inclusions. As many of these short works are aimed at a juvenile audience, only a representative selection of them was included.

Genealogical directories of marriages, parish registers, courthouse records, etc., make up another large segment of the biographical literature. As most of these titles do not provide biographical data, only a representative sampling was included.

One group of sources that we intend to explore more fully in future editions are the nineteenth- and early twentieth-century "vanity" biographical dictionaries. A selection of these titles is included, but as many of them are of local or regional interest, it will take some time to identify them all and provide a full listing of these works. Any assistance that readers can offer in identifying these works would be greatly appreciated.

We also hope that our readers who identify omissions or errors will take the time to notify us of the needed corrections for future inclusions. Send additions and corrections to: Brian Alley/Jennifer Cargill/Diane J. Cimbala; c/o Brian Alley; 2057 South Glenwood Avenue; Springfield, IL 62704.

ARRANGEMENT

The sources listed in this volume are arranged into broad subject categories, which are indicated in the Table of Contents. The Indices provide more detailed subject and author/title access. Within each broad subject area, entries are arranged alphabetically by title. We chose this arrangement in order to group like titles together in the listing, even when authors and editors changed.

REFERENCES

1. *Dictionary of National Biography*, ed. by Sir Leslie Stephen and Sir Sidney Lee. London: Smith, Elder, 1908–09. 22 volumes.

2. Eugene P. Sheehy, *Guide to Reference Books*, 9th ed. Chicago: American Library Association, 1976.

3. *Gale Biographical Index Series*. Detroit, MI: Gale Research Company, 1975.

I. General Sources

WORLDWIDE

1. Potter, George L. *Authentic Biographies of the World's Greatest People*. St. Augustine, FL: Potter's International Hall of Fame, 1955.

Brief biographies are provided for those individuals included in Potter's Wax Museum. Entries provide some biographical data and describe the exploits or contributions of these people. Also included are photographs of the wax figures.

2. *Biographical Encyclopedia of the World*. 2d ed. New York: Institute for Research in Biography, Inc., 1942.

Provides biographical sketches of international leaders. Political and financial figures are emphasized, and photographs accompany some entries. All entries are in English except for those profiling prominent Latin Americans.

3. *The Blue Book: Leaders of the English-Speaking World*. U.K. and Commonwealth ed. Chicago: St. James Press, 1971.

A variation on the "Who's Who" theme. A scope note in the preface describes the work as listing "persons in the United Kingdom, Ireland, Australia, New Zealand, Canada and the United States of America who have achieved distinction in the arts and sciences, business or the professions."

4. Paxton, John, and Fairfield, Sheila. *Calendar of Creative Man*. New York: Facts on File, Inc., 1980 (c1979).

The *Calendar* attempts to trace human beings' creative development chronologically from approximately 500 A.D. to 1970 A.D. Reflecting a Western interpretation of time, the book emphasizes dates and cultures that change slowly. Creativity in all forms appears on these pages from "architecture to needlework...Japanese puppets...[to] the lace glass of Venice...."

Each time period is arranged by nationality, but the work studiously avoids ethnocentrism in coverage. South and Central America, Africa, and the Near and Far East earn equal coverage with European accomplishments.

The volume is arranged chronologically. There is no index, an omission which hampers effective use of the work.

5. Bernstein, Herman. *Celebrities of Our Time: Interviews.* London: Hutchinson and Co., 1924. Reprint. Freeport, NY: Books for Libraries Press, 1968.

> Thirty-one individuals are profiled in chapters drawn from the author's actual discussions with the subjects. These men were all prominent in the early twentieth century when the author had an opportunity to talk with them.

6. Thorne, J.O., and Collocott, T.C. *Chamber's Biographical Dictionary.* Rev. with supplement. Edinburgh: W. & R. Chambers, 1974.

> Over 15,000 precise biographies are included—precise in factual data provided, though some opinions color some entries. The work is international in scope and attempts to cover world history.

7. Hammerton, J.A. *Concise Universal Biography: A Dictionary of the Famous Men and Women of All Countries and All Times Recording the Lives of More Than 20,000 Persons and Profusely Illustrated with Authentic Portraits and Other Pictorial Documents.* 4 volumes in 2. Reprint of 1934–35 ed. London: Educational Book Co., Ltd.; Detroit, MI: Gale, 1975.

> This is a list of personalities living and dead. Twenty thousand entries make up the body of the work, which is based upon the biographical section of the *Universal Encyclopedia.* The entries are brief and are arranged in alphabetical order. Photographs, woodcuts, and line drawings are used extensively throughout the work and are of good quality.

8. Moritz, Charles. *Current Biography Yearbook.* 1984 ed. New York: H. W. Wilson, Inc., 1940–. Annual.

> The purpose of *Current Biography* is to provide brief, accurate, up-to-date articles on leaders in all fields of human accomplishment, as well as obituaries for people previously profiled in *Current Biography.* Almost every profession is represented with each profile running several pages in length, opening with a headnote giving the person's name and the position for which that person is known. Updates appear occasionally for luminaries who have maintained their prominence over the decades. Each entry concludes with citations to the reference and periodical literature in which additional information may be found.
>
> Each annual volume also includes obituaries for those people who were profiled in previous volumes. These, too, include references to obituaries appearing in periodicals and newspapers.
>
> A separate index volume is available for 1940–70. Volumes for 1971–80 include indices cumulative from 1971; volumes from 1981– include indices cumulative from 1981.

9. Phillips, Lawrence B. *Dictionary of Biographical Reference.* London: S. Low, Marston and Co., 1889. Reprint. Detroit, MI: Gale, 1981.

> This reprint of an 1889 work, itself a revision of yet earlier works, profiles 100,000 people in extremely brief coverage. Entries are 1–2 lines long and date back to Adam and Eve. A supplement at the end has a

separate alphabetical arrangement and covers the years 1870–88. A bibliography of biographical works completes the volume.

10. Vincent, Benjamin. *A Dictionary of Biography, Past and Present, Containing the Chief Events in the Lives of Eminent Persons of All Ages and Nations.* London: Ward, Lock and Co., 1877. Reprint. Detroit, MI: Gale, 1974.

The introductory pages contain brief biographies of present rulers, accompanied by genealogical charts for 34 countries or royal houses that were in existence in 1877. For countries such as the U.S., the presidential succession is listed. Many of the royal houses and countries cited either no longer exist or are no longer prominent.

Following these introductory pages is an alphabetical listing of brief biographies of people deemed important in the history of the world through the 1870s.

11. Kay, Ernest. *Dictionary of International Biography: A Biographical Record of Contemporary Achievement.* 5th ed. London: Dictionary of International Biography, 1968.

This edition of *DIB* contains biographical entries in listing form for more than 14,000 people. Entries are very brief, and while many notable people are omitted from the work, a substantial number of obscure individuals are included. Emphasis is on the average educator, civic worker, accountant, or physician.

12. Hyamson, Albert M. *A Dictionary of Universal Biography of All Ages and of All Peoples.* 2d ed. New York: E. P. Dutton, 1951. Reprint. Detroit, MI: Gale, 1981.

Thousands of entries are included in an extremely brief format of 1–2 lines. Entries consist of name, primary occupation, and life dates, as well as an abbreviation that indicates sources where more complete biographies of the subjects may be located.

While the information contained herein is of limited value, Hyamson serves as a guide to more complete biographical sketches.

13. Archer, Jules. *Famous Young Rebels.* New York: Messner, 1973.

Lists biographies of 12 well-known men and women who in their youth were considered to be the radicals of their day. Among the rebels included are Nehru, Elizabeth Gurley Flynn, Marcus Garvey, and Margaret Sanger. [Juvenile]

14. Thomas, Henry, and Thomas, Dana Lee. *50 Great Modern Lives: Inspiring Biographies of Men and Women Who Have Guided Mankind to a Better World.* Garden City, NY: Hanover House, 1956.

The volume contains narrative biographies describing events in the lives of these "road-makers." The biographies are followed by a chronology of major events in each subject's life.

15. *The International Who's Who.* London: Europa Publications Ltd.; Detroit, MI: Gale, 1935–. Biennial.

This 47th edition contains biographies of living individuals prominent in international affairs, government, administration, diplomacy, science, medicine, etc. The edition includes 15,000 listings, 1,000 of which are new. The alphabetical entries include the usual biographical information:

birth date, nationality, area of prominence, education and career information, accomplishments, and current address. A list of reigning monarchs is also provided. Included in this collection of biographies are people in countries for which there is no national *Who's Who*.

16. Weis, Frank W. *Lifelines: Famous Contemporaries from 600 B.C. to 1975.* New York: Facts on File, Inc., 1982.

This work is divided into 25-year time spans describing people active during each period. While there is a brief overview of the period covered, the work's focus is biographical. An index of personal names allows the user access to data on specific individuals.

17. *The McGraw-Hill Encyclopedia of World Biography.* 12 volumes. New York: McGraw-Hill Book Company, 1973.

An illustrated biographical encyclopedia that is international in scope. Entries include a list of additional readings. Volume 12 contains an extensive index and 17 study guides, arranging the entries into geographical and philosophical areas of study.

18. Wintle, Justin. *Makers of Modern Culture.* New York: Facts on File, Inc., 1981.

This is a compilation of biographies on twentieth-century (since 1914) contributors to modern thought, art, and form. Included are fine and performing artists, "philosophers, sociologists, anthropologists, theologians and political theorists," writers, architects, and more. The signed articles vary in length and offer critiques of the individual's contribution to modern culture. A list of works (e.g., bibliography, discography, cinematography) follows most entries. An index of names and key terms provides access not only to individuals, but also to ideas such as "art deco," "fauvism," "cubism," and "totalitarianism."

19. ———. *Makers of Nineteenth Century Culture 1800–1914.* London: Routledge & Kegan Paul, 1982.

Contains signed articles on almost 500 people who are considered, by the editor, to have been influential in the nineteenth century. The articles provide basic biographical data and a discussion of the person's contributions. An index provides subject access.

20. Barnhart, Clarence L., and Halsey, William D. *New Century Cyclopedia of Names.* 3 volumes. New York: Appleton-Century-Crofts, 1954.

The preface to the *New Century Cyclopedia of Names* describes it as: "consisting solely of information about proper names having importance in the English-speaking world." In addition to providing brief biographical information about famous people throughout world history, the *Cyclopedia* includes place names; titles of books; the names of characters in plays, novels, and operas; and names in translation. The 3-volume set is heavily cross-referenced. Entries are similar to those found in many biographical dictionaries: A short description of the individual's notable contribution is preceded by a pronunciation of the person's name and his/her dates of birth and death. Arranged alphabetically, with volume 3 including several appendices, among which are a "Chronological Table of World History" covering prehistory to 1953; a list of heads of state by country (also arranged chronologically); genealogical charts of the rulers of European nations; a table of popes; and a list of prenames used in the work, with pronunciations and national origin.

21. Gunther, John. *Procession: Dominant Personalities of Four Decades as Seen by the Author of the Inside Books.* New York: Harper & Row, 1965.

Some biographies are brief sketches, some are essays, while others are character sketches. The 50 personalities considered to be the most important of the twentieth century are grouped by decades and periods of intense activity.

22. Rawlins, Ray. *The Stein and Day Book of World Autographs.* Briarcliff Manor, NY: Stein and Day, 1978.

Although not technically a biographical source, this work is of potential use to seekers of biographical information. The book is an alphabetical listing of reproduced signatures. All of the autographs belong to famous people, but coverage is international and spans over 1,200 years. Next to each autograph is a short biographical sketch. Cross-references are provided for aliases and pen names.

23. Snyder, Louis L. *A Treasury of Intimate Biographies: Dramatic Stories from the Lives of Great Men Told by Those Who Knew Them Well and Who Themselves Were Men and Women of Distinction in Literature and the Arts.* New York: Greenburg, 1951.

Forty-five individuals are profiled by their contemporaries in material taken from writings of the period in which they lived.

24. *Webster's Biographical Dictionary.* Springfield, MA: G. & C. Merriam Company, 1980.

Included are 40,000 short entries on deceased persons of historical prominence. Pronunciations accompany all names. The scope is international, but British and American individuals dominate the listings.

25. *Webster's New Biographical Dictionary.* Rev. ed. Springfield, MA: Merriam-Webster, Inc., 1983.

This revision of *Webster's Biographical Dictionary* contains biographical information on 30,000 notable figures and spans the last 5,000 years. In addition to the alphabetically arranged biographical entries, there are brief sections devoted to notes, symbols, and abbreviations.

26. Howat, Gerald. *Who Did What: The Lives and Achievements of the 5000 Men and Women—Leaders of Nations, Saints and Sinners, Artists and Scientists—Who Shaped the World.* New York: Crown, 1974.

Brief descriptions of the achievements of 5,000 individuals are included, along with listings by dynasty or state and "A Time Chart of Human Achievement."

27. Palmer, Alan. *Who's Who in Modern History 1860–1980.* New York: Holt, Rinehart and Winston; London: Weidenfeld and Nicholson, 1980.

This is an alphabetical biographical dictionary of leaders who have affected world history since 1860. Persons both living and dead are included. There is no index, but cross-references to proper names from other titles, and from entry to entry, are plentiful. Entries in this "album of short biographies" provide commentary on major events of the period and in the lives of the biographees. An introductory essay is provided, which describes the 120 years covered.

THE ANCIENT WORLD

28. Avery, Catherine. *The New Century Classical Handbook.* New York: Appleton-Century-Crofts, 1962.
  This encyclopedia provides information about the Greek and Roman worlds, starting with prehistoric Greece and ending with first-century Rome. Biographies are included and are written to demonstrate what contemporary Greeks and Romans might have written; legend is not separated from fact. Dates are supplied where possible and highlights of the individual's life comprise the body of most entries.

29. Bowder, Diana. *Who Was Who in the Roman World: 753 BC–AD 476.* Ithaca, NY: Cornell University Press, 1980.
  Gives brief profiles of Roman luminaries from the legendary founding of the city to the fall of the Empire. Includes a chronology, bibliographical references, illustrations, and a glossary.

THE UNITED STATES

30. Briscoe, Mary Louise. *American Autobiography 1945–1980: A Bibliography.* Madison, WI: University of Wisconsin Press, 1982.
  The annotations to the books cited in this bibliography provide brief biographical information, and a subject index provides additional access points.

31. Preston, Wheeler. *American Biographies.* New York: Harper and Row, 1940. Reprint. Detroit, MI: Gale, 1974.
  A dictionary-arranged biographical work consisting of notables in the United States. No living person was included when the book was first published in 1940. Some women are included, and each short entry includes citations to other biographical information.

32. Faber, Harold, and Faber, Doris. *American Heroes of the Twentieth Century.* New York: Random House, 1967.
  The heroes profiled in this volume for young people include 5 women and 2 Blacks. They range from presidents and military leaders to inventors and performing artists. A list for further reading is provided. The index provides subject access. [Juvenile]

33. Wilson, James Grant, et al. *Appleton's Cyclopedia of American Biography.* 7 volumes. New York: D. Appleton, 1888–1918. (6 supplementary volumes were issued in 1918–31; also available as a Gale reprint, 1968.)

> *Appleton's* includes 15,000 prominent U.S. citizens, other figures from the Western hemisphere, and persons who were involved in American history up to the time of compilation. Vital facts are listed for each entry, followed by details of the individual's life in essay form. Major contributions that the person made to history, industry, and the arts are indicated. Both men and women are included. Some entries for fictitious people appear in the compilation.

34. Sabine, Lorenzo. *Biographical Sketches of Loyalists of the American Revolution with an Historical Essay.* 2 volumes. Port Washington, NY: Kennikat Press, 1966. Reprint. Baltimore, MD: Genealogical Publishing, 1979.

> First published in 1864, this 3-part work is a valuable source of information on those who chose loyalty to the crown during this critical period in U.S. history. A lengthy historical essay introduces the subject of the Tories' plight and is followed by the "Biographical Sketches" section, which is quite extensive. An additional section provides brief mention of 1,500 loyalists not included in the biographical sketches.

35. Nash, Jay Robert. *Bloodletters and Badmen: A Narrative Encyclopedia of American Criminals from the Pilgrims to the Present.* New York: M. Evans and Company, 1973.

> The self-explanatory title describes the content of this work. Brief biographical data are given, including a classification of the criminal—murderer, syndicate gangster, or extortionist, for example. For the major criminals, a narrative is included describing in more detail the events, particularly the crimes, of their lives. Also included are entries for gangs, groups (e.g., The Mafia), and events (e.g., the O.K. Corral Shootout).

36. Reeder, "Red" Russell Potter. *Bold Leaders of the American Revolution.* Boston: Little, Brown, 1973.

> This small volume includes 12 short biographies of Revolutionary-era notables. In addition to male colonists, 2 women, 1 Polish engineer, and 2 British sympathizers are profiled. In the geographic distribution, New Englanders dominate though South Carolina's Francis Marion, Michigan's "Mad" Anthony Wayne, and George Rogers Clark of the Old Northwest Territory are also included.

37. Amory, Cleveland. *Celebrity Register: An Irreverent Compendium of American Quotable Notables.* New York: Harper & Row, 1959. Irregular.

> A biographical guide to those whose names "once made by news, now make news by themselves." The short, illustrated entries are gossipy, containing interview excerpts and juicy tidbits about the individual's career, background, and social life. This irregular serial has been edited since 1973 by Earl Blackwell.

38. *Concise Dictionary of American Biography: Complete to 1960.* 3d ed. New York: Charles Scribner's, 1980. (See also *Dictionary of American Biography.*)

> More than 17,000 biographies from the parent set and its supplements were abridged for this concise edition. All are outstanding Americans who died prior to January 1, 1961; individuals must have been dead more than 10 years to be included. There are 3 types of entries: minimal, which give very brief data; median, which provide brief data plus commentary on achievements; and extended, which are narrative in form and are reserved for major figures.

39. Johnson, Allen, and Malone, Dumas, et al. *Dictionary of American Biography.* 20 volumes plus an index volume and periodic supplements. New York: Scribner's, 1928–. (See also *Concise Dictionary of American Biography: Complete to 1960.*)

> Patterned after the esteemed *Dictionary of National Biography,* the *D.A.B.* contains signed biographical sketches on famous deceased Americans. Some personal data are included, unlike the *Who's Who* publications, and the sketches are written in narrative form. A short list of bibliographic materials concludes each entry.
>
> The *D.A.B.* has come under fire in recent years because of its obvious bias in favor of White Anglo-Saxon Protestant men, and against women, ethnics, and minorities. Historians have criticized its use of evaluative terminology and the absence of continuous revision of the entries. Nevertheless, it is a valuable biographical source.

40. Lender, Mark Edward. *Dictionary of American Temperance Biography: From Temperance Reform to Alcohol Research, the 1600s to the 1980s.* Westport, CT: Greenwood, 1984.

> Entries provide basic biographical data, a discussion of the individual's role, and a bibliography of works by or about the person. There is also a subject/name/organization index and lists of birthplaces and religions of the entrants.

41. Garraty, John Arthur. *Encyclopedia of American Biography.* New York: Harper & Row, 1974.

> Contains over 1,000 biographies of living and deceased Americans. Entries are divided into 2 sections: The first provides basic biographical data and the second is a short essay evaluating the individual's contribution to his/her field of endeavor. The signed essays include references to other sources that provide information on the subject.

42. Hawthorne, Nathaniel. *Famous Old People: Being the Second Epoch of Grandfather's Chair.* 2d ed. Boston: Tappan and Dennet, 1842.

> A children's story of Colonial and Revolutionary America, told in narrative form. Politicians, soldiers, and adventurers of the period are highlighted. [Juvenile]

43. Felton, Bruce, and Fowler, Mark. *Felton & Fowler's Famous Americans You Never Knew Existed.* New York: Stein and Day Publishers, 1981.

    A collection of 400 bizarre Americans who have earned (or should have earned) a spot in the annals of American trivia. The book, which is illustrated, is divided into 15 broad categories, such as "Blunderers, Dreamers, and Enthusiasts," "Overdoers," and "Evildoers." Humor is emphasized.

44. Downs, Robert B.; Flanagan, John T.; and Scott, Harold W. *Memorable Americans, 1750–1950.* Littleton, CO: Libraries Unlimited, 1983.

    This ready reference to the lives and contributions of 150 men and women will prove helpful in small collections or home libraries. The sketches provide biographical data as well as listing the biographee's writings and works that will lead to sources of additional information. There are also appendices listing the men and women by career field and birth date.

45. Phelps, Robert H. *Men in the News: Biographical Sketches from The New York Times.* Philadelphia, PA: J.B. Lippincott Company, 1959.

    This irregular serial contains summaries of biographies appearing as news items in the *New York Times.*

46. *National Cyclopedia of American Biography.* New York: James T. White and Co., 1888–.

    This work is "Edited by Distinguished Biographers, Selected from Each State. Revised and Approved by the Most Eminent Historians, Scholars, and Statesmen of the Day." The work appears in a Permanent Series, which is never revised, and a Current Series, which is ongoing. Entries in the multivolume *National Cyclopedia* are derived from information supplied by family members and close acquaintances, as well as the "distinguished biographers" credited on the title page of early volumes. Detailed and heavily illustrated, the *National Cyclopedia* contains portraits of those profiled and drawings of the subjects' residences and monuments, as well as other pertinent illustrations.

    It is necessary to use the indices to gain access to the entries since there is no logical order to the arrangement. Despite the obvious biases in a biographical work constructed in this manner, the *National Cyclopedia* is an invaluable reference source.

47. Smith, William. *The National Register of Prominent Americans and International Notables.* 1974–75 ed. Venice, FL: The National Register of Prominent Americans and International Notables, 1974–75.

    A state-by-state membership directory of prominent men and women of the Association. Membership is by invitation, and only living persons are included in the directory. At the end of each state listing is an index of names arranged by profession and a separate alphabetical list of those willing to serve as speakers or lecturers.

48. Shipton, Clifford K. *New England Life in the 18th Century;
Representative Biographies from Sibley's Harvard Graduates.*
Cambridge, MA: Belknap Press of Harvard University Press, 1963.
(See also *Sibley's Harvard Graduates.*)
  Clifford K. Shipton continued the series begun by John Langdon Sibley
  as *Sibley's Harvard Graduates.* These representative biographies are of 60
  Harvard graduates or honorary graduates, such as George Washington,
  from the Class of 1690, to the Class of 1750.

49. *Notable Names in American History: A Tabulated Register.*
Clifton, NJ: James T. White & Co., 1973.
  This is the third edition of a work originally entitled *White's Conspectus
  of American Biography.* In it, names of prominent U.S. citizens are
  grouped by era (e.g., The Colonial Era) or branch of government (e.g.,
  the Cabinet), states, and area of interest (e.g., higher education, organized labor). An index is provided to the 50,000 entries.

50. Beard, Annie E. S. *Our Foreign-Born Citizens.* 6th ed. New York:
Crowell, 1968.
  Chapter-length biographical sketches of 23 men who immigrated to
  America and subsequently made a substantial contribution to society.
  Several native nationalities are represented, as are a variety of careers,
  ranging from poet W. H. Auden to architect Walter Gropius and includ-
  ing medical researcher Hideyo Noguchi. An index provides access to
  names and concepts. [Juvenile]

51. *Personalities of America.* 2d ed. Raleigh, NC: American
Biographical Institute, 1983.
  The American Biographical Institute publishes several regional biographical dictionaries of contemporary Americans. *Personalities of America* is a
  compilation derived from the most influential people profiled in the
  regional titles.

52. Shipton, Clifford K. *Sibley's Harvard Graduates: Biographical
Sketches of Those Who Attended Harvard College....* Boston:
Massachusetts Historical Society, 1975.
  This series was begun in 1859 by John Langdon Sibley, a librarian at
  Harvard. It was revived by Shipton, a Harvard archivist and director
  and librarian of the American Antiquarian Society. Each volume is
  arranged by graduating class and then alphabetically by name. The
  completed volumes are particularly useful in the area of early U.S.
  history and genealogy.

53. *Significant Americans.* 16 volumes. Chicago: Childrens Press,
1976.
  For grades 4–12. Different volumes cover different fields of interest or
  groups of people. [Juvenile]

54. Van Doren, Charles, and McHenry, Robert. *Webster's American
Biographies.* Springfield, MA: G. & C. Merriam, 1984.
  Over 3,000 biographies of living and deceased Americans. All professions
  are included, as represented by the "Careers and Professions Index." A
  geographical index is also included.

55. Brown, Dee. *The Westerners.* New York: Holt, Rinehart and Winston, 1974.

An excellent historical survey of the American West from the point of view of selected individuals who exemplify the Western spirit. They range in time period from the sixteenth to the twentieth centuries and include such diverse members as D.H. Lawrence, Sitting Bull, Cabeza de Vaca, and Lewis and Clark.

The book is arranged into chronological chapters and is heavily illustrated with photographs and paintings of Westerners and the West. Full captions and citations for the illustrations appear near the end of the book, along with a map of the western United States and a chapter-by-chapter bibliography. The index provides access to both the text and illustrations.

56. *Who Was Who during the American Revolution.* Compiled by Editors of *Who's Who in America* with Jerry Kail. Indianapolis, IN: Bobbs-Merrill, 1976.

Fifteen hundred people, some of whom had very peripheral contact with the Revolution, are listed in the briefest of entries.

Who Was Who in America has several volumes that are component volumes of the "Who's Who in American History" series. The issued volumes follow:

57. *Who Was Who in America: Historical Volume 1607–1896.* Rev. ed. Chicago: Marquis Who's Who, 1967.

This volume covers the period from the founding of the Jamestown Virginia Colony to 1897. Prefatory material covers presidents, vice presidents, and elected officials of the United States; a time line chart; state name origins; statistical and historical data on principal U.S. cities; and a listing of major events in U.S. history. Approximately 13,250 biographical sketches are included.

58. *Who Was Who in America 1897–1942.* Chicago: Marquis Who's Who, 1968.

Contains the names of 25,000 biographees removed from *Who's Who in America* volumes because they died.

59. *Who Was Who in America 1943–1950.* Chicago: Marquis Who's Who, 1950.

Contains the names of 8,400 biographees removed from *Who's Who in America* because they died.

60. *Who Was Who in America 1951–1960.* Chicago: Marquis Who's Who, 1960.

Contains the names of 12,828 biographees removed from *Who's Who in America* volumes because they died.

61. *Who Was Who in America 1961–1968.* Chicago: Marquis Who's Who, 1968.

Contains the names of 16,000 biographees removed from *Who's Who in America* because they died. In addition, the volume contains an index of the 80,000 names appearing in *Who Was Who in America* volumes issued to date.

62. *Who Was Who in America with World Notables 1969–1973.* Chicago: Marquis Who's Who, 1973; *Who Was Who in America with World Notables 1974–1976.* Chicago: Marquis Who's Who, 1976; *Who Was Who in America with World Notables 1977–1981.* Chicago: Marquis Who's Who, 1981.

The preceding 3 volumes contain the biographies of deceased persons who, when living, were profiled in *Who's Who in America* or other prominent sources. Selected international figures who had an impact on American history are also included, as are sketches on people known to be 95 years old or more.

63. *Who Was Who in America with World Notables Index 1607–1981.* Chicago: Marquis Who's Who, 1981.

Lists names of biographees, from the historical volume issued for 1607–1896 through the seventh volume covering the years 1977–81.

64. *Who's Who in America.* Chicago: Marquis Who's Who. Biannual.

Students trying to decide if *Who's Who in America* will contain a biography of an individual would do well to read the "Standards of Admission" that appear near the front of each volume. The "Standards" list the occupations of people most likely to appear in the volume and acknowledge that distinctive personal achievement can win a spot in the work for exceptional individuals. Thus, celebrities of all kinds appear next to Cabinet members, judges, corporate chief executive officers, and major religious leaders.

Other valuable portions include a necrology of individuals who died the previous year and an index of biographees appearing in the *Who's Who* regional directories.

The Confederacy

As this section of the United States was once considered a separate nation, we have created a subsection for biographical sources on the Confederate States of America.

65. Wakelyn, Jon L., and Vandiver, Frank E. *Biographical Dictionary of the Confederacy.* Westport, CT: Greenwood Press, 1977.

This collection of biographical sketches covers the careers of a variety of leaders in the Confederacy during the period of the Civil War. The entries are preceded by 4 introductory chapters discussing the criteria for selecting biographees, prewar career patterns of biographees, their wartime activities, and their leadership in the post-war period. Includes approximately 600 biographical sketches, written in narrative form and including sources.

66. Warner, Ezra J., and Yearns, W. Buck. *Biographical Register of the Confederate Congress.* Baton Rouge, LA: Louisiana State University Press, 1975.

An introduction details the formation of the Confederate Congress and how that body functioned during the Civil War. Included in the essay is a discussion of the congressmen's relationship to Jefferson Davis (president of the Confederacy), an analysis of their careers, and an indication of the extent of their slave holdings. Many of the congressmen were obscure before the war and returned to obscurity after the war ended. Thus, extensive research was necessary in compiling these biographies.

The biographical data are in narrative form, beginning with place and date of birth, followed by a discussion of the individuals' careers and personal lives. The degree of their political activities is also indicated. Appendices include: I. a listing of the sessions of the Confederate Congress; II. a list of the standing committees; III. membership of the Congresses, grouped by state and by senators and representatives; and IV. maps of the Confederacy. There are illustrations and a bibliography.

Genealogy-Related Sources to American Biographies

Numerous volumes have been issued that provide genealogical data sources and assist in the compilation of biographies. Following are a few samples of this genre. These titles are not annotated because they are usually no more than lists of names and dates. They show ancestral relationships but provide no further biographical information. (See also *Biography and Genealogy Master Index: A Consolidated Index to More than 3,200,000 Biographical Sketches in Over 350 Current and Retrospective Biographical Dictionaries.*)

67. Coldham, Peter Wilson. *Bonded Passengers to America.* 9 volumes in 3. Baltimore, MD: Genealogical Publishing, 1982. (See also *Burke's Genealogical and Heraldic History of the Peerage, Baronetage, and Knightage.*)

68. Hardy, Stella Pickett. *Colonial Families of the Southern States of America: A History and Genealogy of Colonial Families Who Settled in the Colonies Prior to the Revolution.* 2d ed. Baltimore, MD: Southern Book Co., 1958. Reprint. Baltimore, MD: Genealogical Publishing Co., 1981.

69. Clark, Murtie June. *Colonial Soldiers of the South 1732–1774.* Baltimore, MD: Genealogical Publishing, 1983.

70. Dobson, David. *Directory of Scots Banished to the American Plantations, 1650–1775.* Baltimore, MD: Genealogical Publishing, 1983.

71. Scott, Kenneth. *Early New York Naturalizations.* Baltimore, MD: Genealogical Publishing, 1981.

72. Greer, George Cabell. *Early Virginia Immigrants, 1623–1666.* Baltimore, MD: Genealogical Publishing, 1982.

73. Dobson, David. *English Estates of American Settlers: American Wills and Administrations in the Prerogative Court of Canterbury, 1800–1858.* Baltimore, MD: Genealogical Publishing, 1981.

74. Glazier, Ira A., and Tepper, Michael H. *The Famine Immigrants: Lists of Irish Immigrants Arriving at the Port of New York, 1846–1851. Volume I: January 1846–1847; Volume II: July 1847–June 1848.* 2 volumes. Baltimore, MD: Genealogical Publishing, 1983.

75. Dawson, Nelson L. *The Filson Club History Quarterly.* Louisville, KY: The Filson Club, 1930–. (See also *Genealogies of Kentucky Families: Family History Articles from The Register of the Kentucky Historical Society and the Filson Club History Quarterly.*)
    A history journal dealing with Kentucky's heritage, as well as other surrounding states, the *Quarterly* emphasizes biographical articles, although pieces on other historical subjects are included.

76. Savage, James. *A Genealogical Dictionary of the First Settlers of New England,* 1977. Reprint. Baltimore, MD: Genealogical Publishing, 1981.

77. *Genealogies of Kentucky Families: Family History Articles from The Register of the Kentucky Historical Society and The Filson Club History Quarterly.* 3 volumes. Baltimore, MD: Genealogical Publishing, 1981. (See also *Filson Club History Quarterly.*)

78. *Genealogies of Pennsylvania Families: Family History Articles from The Pennsylvania Magazine of History and Biography.* Baltimore, MD: Genealogical Publishing, 1981.

79. *Genealogies of Virginia Families: Family History Articles from The Virginia Magazine of History and Biography.* 5 volumes. Baltimore, MD: Genealogical Publishing, 1981.

80. *Genealogies of Virginia Families from Tyler's Quarterly Historical and Genealogical Magazine.* 4 volumes. Baltimore, MD: Genealogical Publishing, 1981.

81. Bentley, Elizabeth Petty. *Index to the 1820 Census of Tennessee.* Baltimore, MD: Genealogical Publishing, 1981.

82. Holbrook, Jay Mack. *New Hampshire 1732 Census.* Oxford, MA: Holbrook Research Institute, 1981.

83. Brandow, James C. *Omitted Chapters from Hotten's Original Lists of Persons of Quality.* Baltimore, MD: Genealogical Publishing, 1982. (See also *Passenger and Immigration Lists Index: A Guide to Published Arrival Records of About 500,000 Passengers Who Came to the United States and Canada in the Seventeenth, Eighteenth, and Nineteenth Centuries.*)

84. Pope, Charles Henry. *The Pioneers of Massachusetts (1620–1650): A Descriptive List Drawn from Records of the Colonies, Towns, and Churches.* Baltimore, MD: Genealogical Publishing, 1981.

85. Holbrook, Brent E. *South Carolina Marriages, 1800–1820.* Baltimore, MD: Genealogical Publishing, 1981.

86. *Virginia Land Records.* Baltimore, MD: Genealogical Publishing, 1982.

87. *Virginia Marriage Records.* Baltimore, MD: Genealogical Publishing, 1982.

88. *Virginia Vital Records.* Baltimore, MD: Genealogical Publishing, 1982.

89. Torrence, Clayton. *Virginia Wills and Administrations 1632–1800.* 1978. Reprint. Baltimore, MD: Genealogical Publishing, 1981.

90. *Virginia Wills Records.* Baltimore, MD: Genealogical Publishing, 1982.

91. Meyer, Mary Keysor, and Filby, P. William. *Who's Who in Genealogy and Heraldry. Volume I.* Detroit, MI: Gale, 1981.
Several hundred specialists in genealogy and heraldry are listed in this compilation and were selected based on contributions to the field, significant achievement in the field, and public interest in the biography subject. Each entry includes the usual biographical information, career activities, genealogical publications, and special interests.

THE UNITED KINGDOM

92. Valentine, Alan. *The British Establishment 1760–1784: An Eighteenth Century Biographical Dictionary.* 2 volumes. Norman, OK: University of Oklahoma Press, 1970.
In his foreword, author Valentine explains: "The period 1760 to 1784 was chosen because that interval is one of special interest to both British and American historians, because it has a remarkable if often painful unity in its problems...." Included are men at court; in the government, military, church, legal, and financial professions; and those whose reputations place them in "society."

93. *The Concise Dictionary of National Biography.* See *The Dictionary of National Biography: The Concise Dictionary* (96).

94. Boylan, Henry. *A Dictionary of Irish Biography.* New York: Barnes and Noble, 1978.
Contains biographies of deceased residents (by birth or adoption) of Ireland. Arranged alphabetically, the work is patterned after the *Dictionary of National Biography* and includes some legendary personae, as well as those more easily verified.

95. Stephen, Sir Leslie, and Lee, Sir Sidney. *The Dictionary of National Biography.* 22 volumes. London: Oxford University Press, 1885-1900.

The first 21 volumes contain biographies of 29,120 men and women (British and Irish) who have received any distinction of importance during their careers. The period covered is from earliest recorded history to 1900. Volume 22 contains 1,000 articles, of which 200 represent omissions from the basic 21-volume set.

The Dictionary of National Biography, a classic among biographical works, has been supplemented by additional volumes and edited by several different people. A listing of these volumes follows. Each volume covers prominent Britons who died during the years specified in the title.

Lee, Sir Sidney. *The Dictionary of National Biography, 1901-1911.* 3 volumes in 1. London: Oxford University Press, 1912; Davis, H. W. C., and Weaver, J. R. H. *The Dictionary of National Biography, 1912-1921.* London: Oxford University Press, 1927.

Includes an index covering the years 1901-21.

Weaver, J. R. H. *The Dictionary of National Biography, 1922-1930.* London: Oxford University Press, 1937.

Includes a cumulative index covering 1901-30.

Legg, L. G. Wickham. *The Dictionary of National Biography, 1931-1940.* London: Oxford University Press, 1949.

Index is cumulative for 1901-40.

Legg, L. G. Wickham, and Williams, E. T., *The Dictionary of National Biography, 1941-1950.* London: Oxford University Press, 1959; Williams, E. T., and Palmer, Helen M. *The Dictionary of National Biography, 1951-1960.* London: Oxford University Press, 1971; Williams, E. T., and Nicholls, C. S. *The Dictionary of National Biography, 1961-1970.* Oxford: Oxford University Press, 1981.

96. *The Dictionary of National Biography: The Concise Dictionary.* 2 volumes. London: Oxford University Press, 1961.

Volume 2 contains "the epitome" of the entries covered in the *Dictionary of National Biography* through Queen Victoria's death on January 22, 1901. Volume 2 covers the period 1901-50 and includes selected obituaries published in the first 5 volumes of *The Twentieth Century D.N.B..* There is a short subject index at the end of each volume.

97. *Famous Men of Britain.* Pease's ed. Albany, NY: Steele and Durrie, 1848.

A tiny children's book, *Famous Men of Britain* devotes one page to each short sketch about a famous Briton. The facing page features a pen-and-ink sketch of the person. Those profiled are mostly major British clergymen (i.e., the Venerable Bede) or royalty.

98. Gould, William. *Lives of the Georgian Age 1714-1837.* New York: Barnes and Noble, 1978.

The preface to this work states that it "contains approximately 300 short biographies of eminent men and women of the Georgian or Hanoverian period from 1714 to 1837." Most subjects are British, although some foreigners whose residence became Great Britain are also included. Colonial Britons living in America are included, but Revolutionary leaders are omitted.

99. *Who's Who: An Annual Biographical Dictionary.* New York: St. Martin's Press, 1849–. Annual.
This massive, premier biographical annual lists prominent individuals from the United Kingdom. An obituary lists notables who died during the previous year, and there is a genealogy of living members of the Royal Family.

100. Palmer, Alan, and Palmer, Victoria. *Who's Who in Shakespeare's England.* New York: St. Martin's Press, 1981.
Concise biographical information is provided for 700 individuals prominent in England from 1590 to 1623.

CANADA

101. Simpson, Kieran. *Canadian Who's Who.* Toronto: University of Toronto Press, 1985. Annual.
This single annual volume contains brief biographical sketches of more than 8,000 prominent Canadians. Biographees are listed alphabetically.

102. *Dictionary of Canadian Biography.* 11 volumes. Toronto: University of Toronto Press (French edition published by Les Presses de L'Universite Laval), 1966–.
This Canadian equivalent of *The Dictionary of National Biography* and *The Dictionary of American Biography* was financed by a bequest from James Nicholson, a Canadian businessperson who was a great admirer of *D.N.B.* and who felt Canada needed a similar national biography. Work began on the project in 1959 with publication of the first volume in 1966. Each volume covers a specific time period with volume 1 covering the years 1000–1700; later volumes cover shorter time sequences: volume 2, 1701–40; volume 3, 1741–70; volume 4, 1771–1800; volume 9, 1861–70; volume 10, 1871–80; volume 11, 1881–90. There is an index for volumes 1–4 and 9–11. Volumes are issued as completed rather than in sequence. Each volume is self-contained since it covers a specific number of years. As more recent years are covered, the volumes will possibly cover less than a decade. Perhaps 20 volumes eventually will be issued.
　　Most volumes include some introductory essays or background information pertinent to the time period. Each entry begins with the usual pertinent biographical facts and then is followed by a narrative describing the individual's life and career. Source notes accompany each entry. A general bibliography is in each volume as is a detailed index. The index volumes contain occupation and geographical indices as well as a list of biographies and a cumulative nominal index listing the names of other people mentioned in the volumes.

103. Wallace, W. Stewart. *The Macmillan Dictionary of Canadian Biography.* 4th ed., rev. enl. Toronto: Macmillan, 1978.
Contains more than 5,000 entries of prominent Canadians who died prior to 1976. Brief biographical data are included plus a bibliography for each entry.

AUSTRALIA

104. Pike, Douglas, et al. *Australian Dictionary of Biography.* 12 volumes planned. Carlton, Victoria, Australia: Melbourne University Press, 1966–.
Prominent Australians and people whose lives were examples of the "Australian Experience" are included in this multivolume work (9 volumes published so far). The set is divided into periods with individuals being placed in the period when most of the person's most important activities occurred. The chronological division was chosen to make compilation easier. All entries are for deceased persons. Several editors have worked on the set. The coverage is: volumes 1–2, 1788–1850; volumes 3–6, 1851–90; volumes 7–8, 1891–1939.
Over 7,000 entries are anticipated when the last volume is published. A National Committee was created to plan and coordinate the massive compilation effort. Working Parties in each state prepared lists of names for possible inclusion.
The entries are very readable, and many are quite lively. Many of the people profiled led colorful lives, having gone to Australia after first encountering difficulties in other countries. Some entries also discuss the lives of spouses, offspring, and events peripheral to the subject. Sources of information are indicated with each entry.

105. Serle, Percival. *Dictionary of Australian Biography.* 2 volumes. Sydney, Australia: Angus and Robertson, 1954.
Australian figures of prominence are included in entries researched and written by the author. All subjects are deceased. A readable narrative discusses the individual's career and personal life. The chief sources used are indicated at the end of each entry. In the preface, Serle discusses other Australian biographical works, who they included, and how they were compiled.

SELECTED OTHER REGIONS

106. Klein, Donald W., and Clark, Anne B. *Biographic Dictionary of Chinese Communism 1921–1965.* 2 volumes. Cambridge, MA: Harvard University Press, 1971.
Individuals selected for inclusion come primarily from pre–1949 China. Over 80 percent of the biographees were alive in 1969; the cutoff date is early 1965. (Because of the Cultural Revolution, access to information on Communist Chinese leaders became scarce, hence the 1965 cutoff date.

The editors confirmed that at least 80 percent of the subjects were still alive in 1969.) Biographees include cabinet ministers; provincial Party secretaries, governors, commanders, and political commissars; ambassadors; leaders of mass organizations, and members of Party control and discipline organizations; ideologues; and the military. The 433 entries are arranged alphabetically with a brief listing of vital statistics followed by a detailed narrative. Each entry includes references to works by and about the biographical sources used for the biography. The second volume contains a selected bibliography, a glossary, and a name index. The appendix includes 96 separate sections that arrange the biographies into every conceivable category.

107. Boorman, Howard L., and Howard, Richard C. *Biographical Dictionary of Republican China.* 5 volumes. New York: Columbia University Press, 1967–71.
    The editors of *BDRC* state that "A minimum goal for the *Biographical Dictionary of Republican China* was the compilation of an accurate chronology of the life of each person whose biography was to be included." The *BDRC* was compiled and edited in the United States. Entries are unsigned for 3 reasons. One was for the sake of discretion since many contributors incorporated personal information and their own experiences. A second reason was the necessity of translating and drastically editing the entries. Finally, some rewriting was necessary in order to ensure objectivity.
    Entries are narratives with the usual biographical data beginning each entry. Chinese characters repeat the name. After a brief listing of biographical data, the narrative details the career and personal life of each subject.
    A general bibliography, which also includes a Chinese translation, ends each volume. The preface in the first volume is an interesting discussion of the difficulty of compiling a work about such a tumultuous period. More than half of volume 4 is a bibliography listing the works used in preparing each entry. The slim fifth volume is the name index.

108. Lazitch, Branko, in collaboration with Milorad M. Drachkovitch. *Biographical Dictionary of the Comintern.* Stanford, CA: Hoover Institution Press, 1973.
    According to Lazitch, "this Dictionary is conceived as an indispensable supplement to that two-volume history of the Comintern under Lenin." Selected for inclusion were: (1) individuals who spoke at Comintern congresses during the years 1919–35 or delegates to the enlarged plenary meetings of the Executive Committee during the years 1922–33 or who played important roles in their countries or in the Comintern; (2) members of the Comintern "apparatus"; (3) leaders of the international organizations associated with the Comintern; and (4) graduates of the 4 principal Comintern schools. These selection criteria resulted in the inclusion of 718 people, with the data current to April 1969. The narratives are alphabetical in arrangement and contain the usual basic biographical information, the political biography for the person within the Party, and the political biography within the Comintern. There is also a list of pseudonyms used.

109. Kay, Ernest. *Dictionary of Latin American and Caribbean Biography.* 2d ed. London: Melrose Press, 1971.
    The foreword of this work states that its aims are to spread information about men and women of the entire Latin American and Caribbean areas through the world in order to assist in development and understanding of the area and its people. Sketches are brief and feature people living at the time of publication.

110. Alexander, Robert J. *Prophets of the Revolution: Profiles of Latin American Leaders.* New York: Macmillan, 1962.
    Profiles of 12 men who influenced or led revolutions in their countries, beginning with Jose Battelle y Ordonez and ending with Fidel Castro.

111. Schultz, Heinrich E.; Urban, Paul K.; and Lebed, Andrew I. *Who Was Who in the USSR: A Biographic Directory Containing 5,015 Biographies of Prominent Soviet Historical Personalities.* Metuchen, NJ: Scarecrow, 1972.
    This work deals with persons no longer living and includes biographies of dissidents and exiles. It covers the period from 1917 to 1967 and includes biographies of persons who have made significant contributions in the areas of political, intellectual, scientific, social, and economic life in the USSR. Biographies are arranged alphabetically. Also included are a guide to the transliteration system used and an index arranged by career and profession.

112. Hilton, Ronald. *Who's Who in Latin America: A Biographical Dictionary of Notable Living Men and Women of Latin America.* 3d ed. rev. and enl. Stanford, CA: Stanford University Press; Chicago: Marquis, 1951.
    Seven volumes of then-current biography, divided into geographical volumes as follows: volume 1, Mexico; volume 2, Central America and Panama; volume 3, Colombia, Ecuador, and Venezuela; volume 4, Bolivia, Chile, and Peru; volume 5, Argentina, Paraguay, and Uruguay; volume 6, Brazil; volume 7, Cuba, the Dominican Republic, and Haiti.

113. *Who's Who in Saudi Arabia 1978–79.* 2d ed. London: Europa Publications; Detroit, MI: Gale Research, 1979.
    Following narrative biographies of the King of Saudi Arabia, the Crown Prince, and the Second Deputy Prime Minister is an alphabetical listing of brief factual entries of the influential people in the country. Most are prominent in government, business, or education. These biographies comprise two-thirds of the book with the last third being a survey essay on Saudi Arabia, complete with charts. Finally, there is a listing of cabinet members and an index arranged by occupation.

114. Bartke, Wolfgang. *Who's Who in the People's Republic of China.* Armonk, NY: M.E. Sharpe, 1981.
    This "reference guide to the current active leadership of China" traces the careers of government officials and Party leaders who held power in the early 1980s, as well as listing those deceased or recently purged from the party. Photos are included whenever possible. Entries are written in narrative form up through October 1949 and assume a chronological listing form for the remaining years. Data were compiled from official

government and Party news sources and publications, as well as archival records in Hong Kong and Taiwan. An appendix maps out the organizational structure of the People's Republic of China, and a conversion table assists readers familiar with the older Wade-Giles transliterations by listing the new Pinyin versions.

115. Lewytzkyi, Borys, and Stroynowski, Juliusz. *Who's Who in the Socialist Countries: A Biographical Encyclopedia of 10,000 Leading Personalities in 16 Communist Countries.* New York: K.G. Saur Publishing Co., 1978.

Contains biographies of leaders from the USSR and 15 other Socialist countries. Unlike comparable Western-type publications, the editors of this work were unable to solicit completed questionnaires from their subjects. Data were gathered from Eastern Bloc reference works, news media, and other sources. Although politicians and party leaders dominate the text, individuals of note in other areas (economics, literature, the arts, science, the military, and religion) are represented. Entries are in traditional "Who's Who" format.

116. *Who's Who in the United Nations and Related Agencies.* New York: Arno Press, 1975.

Covers United Nations and peripheral agency personnel as of 1974, including Secretariat staff, members of permanent missions, executive boards, governing councils or similar bodies, the International Court of Justice, living presidents of the UN General Assembly, and others. Two reference sections provide additional information, including "data about the United Nations System and its personnel" and a directory of UN offices around the world.

GENERAL GUIDES TO NICKNAMES AND PSEUDONYMS

117. Shankle, George Earlie. *American Nicknames: Their Origin and Significance.* 2d ed. New York: H. W. Wilson, 1955.

This revision contains material from the first edition plus additional information. Men, women, cities, states, academic institutions, teams, and other subjects are listed with explanations of how the nicknames were acquired. Nicknames are also included in separate entries.

Entries are narrative, and many include source material at the end. After a heading indicating the person or subject, the narrative states the nickname and discusses its origin. Arrangement is alphabetical, with cross-references from nickname to subject and vice versa. The original compilation was done at the Library of Congress over a 3-year period.

118. Sifakis, Carl. *The Dictionary of Historic Nicknames: A Treasury of More than 7,500 Famous and Infamous Nicknames from World History.* New York: Facts on File, 1984.

A biographical dictionary of famous nickname-bearers, from Abbas "The Bloodshedder" (721?–754) to "The Darling of the Gods" (Tallulah Bankhead), and including the Real McCoy (Bootlegger William McCoy, 1877–1948). Coverage is international and extensive. People carrying several sobriquets have cross-references from each to their given names, followed by a short biographical paragraph describing the circumstances under which the person earned his/her nicknames.

119. Sharp, Harold S. *Handbook of Pseudonyms and Personal Nicknames.* 2 volumes. Metuchen, NJ: Scarecrow, 1972.
A cross-reference guide to authors' pseudonyms and the nicknames of other people. With each person's given name are their life dates and profession. A 2-volume supplement was published in 1975, and a third supplement volume was published in 1982.

120. Mossman, Jennifer. *Pseudonyms and Nicknames Dictionary.* 2d ed. Detroit, MI: Gale Research, 1982.
On the title page of the second edition is the following lengthy subtitle which accurately describes the book: "A Guide to Aliases, Appellations, Assumed Names, Code Names, Cognomens, Cover Names, Epithets, Initialisms, Nicknames, Noms de Guerre, Noms de Plume, Pen Names, Pseudonyms, Sobriquets, and Stage Names of Contemporary and Historical Persons. Including the Subjects' Real Names, Basic Biographical Information, and Citations for the Sources from Which the Entries were Compiled."
    The work contains almost 40,000 original and over 50,000 assumed names of contemporary as well as historical persons. Names are listed alphabetically. Nicknames have cross-references to original names, where the individual's primary occupation and all assumed names are listed, as well as an abbreviation for the biographical source used to obtain the information. A periodic supplement, entitled *New Pseudonyms and Nicknames*, is published irregularly.

121. Frey, Albert R. *Sobriquets and Nicknames.* 1888. Reprint. Detroit, MI: Gale Research, 1966.
A dictionary of nicknames belonging to figures both real and fictitious. Only nicknames are included; there is no way to look up a given name to see what sobriquets that person carried. An explanation for the source of the nickname accompanies each entry.

122. Urdang, Laurence; Kidney, Walter C.; and Kohn, George C. *Twentieth Century American Nicknames.* New York: H.W. Wilson, 1979.
Listed nicknames indicate the person known by that moniker. Entries for the actual person include brief biographical data and other nicknames given that person.

OBITUARIES

123. *The Annual Obituary.* Chicago: St. James Press. Annual.
Entries appear chronologically by date of death. Indices of entrants provide access. There is also an index by profession. Three groups of people are included: people of historical significance, those who have achieved international prominence in their field, and those who are nationally prominent because of their work or a position they have held.

124. Dickerson, Robert B., Jr. *Final Placement: A Guide to the Deaths, Funerals, and Burials of Notable Americans.* Algonac, MI: Reference Publications, 1982.
　　The title describes the contents. Included are 312 people from all walks of life. Brief facts about each are given, as are last words (when known) and other interesting facts about the death, funeral, and burial of each individual.

125. Donaldson, Norman, and Donaldson, Betty. *How Did They Die? The Last Days, Words, Afflictions and Resting Places of Over 300 Notables Throughout History.* New York: St. Martin's Press, 1980.
　　Arranged alphabetically, *How Did They Die?* is just what its title says it is. Emphasizing American and Western European figures, entries cover everyone from Geoffrey Chaucer to Tecumseh to Babe Ruth. The information included here is usually medical and will appeal to curious and hypochondriac readers, as well as those seeking complete biographical information. About half of the entries include photographs.

126. *New York Times Obituaries Index.* New York: New York Times, 1970–.
　　A name index to obituaries in the *New York Times.* Volume 1 covers the years 1858–1968.

127. Roberts, Frank C. *Obituaries from the Times: Including an Index to All Obituaries and Tributes Appearing in the Times during the Years.* (Each volume differs here with the appropriate date, such as 1961–70.) 3 volumes. Reading, England: Newspaper Archive Developments, Ltd., 1975–79.
　　Approximately 4,000 full-text obituaries are covered in these 3 volumes: volume 1, 1951–60; volume 2, 1961–70; and volume 3, 1971–75. Sixty percent of the entries are British. Appendices include a guide to subjects and a general index.

128. Levy, Felice. *Obituaries on File.* 2 volumes. New York: Facts on File, 1979.
　　Nearly 25,000 obituaries that have appeared in *Facts on File* from late 1940 through 1978 are contained here. The 2-volume work is broken down into obituaries, a chronological index of death dates of the men and women cited in the work, and a comprehensive subject index. Obituaries are no longer than one sentence in length.

GUIDES, INDICES, AND LISTS

129. *Biographical Books, 1876–1949.* New York: R. R. Bowker, 1983.
　　This reference tool has the same arrangement as the similar work covering the period 1950–80. It includes full bibliographic data for more than 40,000 entries under biographees and LC subject headings in the name/subject index. There are also author, vocation, geographical, and title indices.

130. *Biographical Books, 1950–1980.* New York: R. R. Bowker, 1980.
Arrangement is alphabetical by name/subject, author, and title in 3 separate listings. Also included is a vocation index listing names/subjects under vocation plus a listing of biographical books in print and a directory of publishers.

131. Slocum, Robert B. *Biographical Dictionaries and Related Works.* 3 volumes. Detroit, MI: 1967, 1972, 1978.
This is an attempt to manage works of collective biography into a master bibliographical listing including biobibliographies, collections of epitaphs, genealogical works, dictionaries of anonyms and pseudonyms, and a variety of other related sources. More than 12,000 entries are included in the 3 volumes. Entries consist of a brief bibliographical citation and short annotations. The main body of the work is broken down into 3 basic segments: Universal Biography, consisting of Bibliography Indexes, Portrait Catalogs, Anonyms and Pseudonyms, Dictionaries and Bio-Bibliographies, etc.; National or Area Biography, consisting of entries arranged alphabetically with geographic areas; and Biography by Vocation, consisting of subjects from Art to Technology. There are separate indices for author, title, and subject access.

132. *Biographical Dictionaries Master Index: A Guide to More than 715,000 Listings in Over Fifty Current Who's Who and Other Works of Collective Biography.* 3 volumes plus supplements. Detroit, MI: Gale, 1975-76.
Entries are simply name, life dates, and sources of the biographies. The source codes themselves give the full bibliographical information for the sources. Continued by *Biography and Genealogy Master Index....*

133. Herbert, Miranda C., and McNeil, Barbara. *Biography and Genealogy Master Index: A Consolidated Index to More than 3,200,000 Biographical Sketches in Over 350 Current and Retrospective Biographical Dictionaries.* 2d ed. 8 volumes. (Also includes supplements, 1981/82, 1983, 1984, 1985). Detroit, MI: Gale, 1980.
The "most comprehensive guide to biographical information ever published." Coverage includes current and retrospective biographical dictionaries. The 350 sources indexed are biographical dictionaries, subject encyclopedias, and works of literary criticism. While the United States is emphasized, works on foreign countries are also indexed. Entries contain the name, life dates, and codes for the sources where biographies can be found. Full bibliographical listings of sources are included.
    Supplements published from 1981–82 to 1985 have indexed nearly 300 additional sources and have added approximately 2,260,000 citations.

134. McNeil, Barbara, and Herbert, Miranda C. *Historical Biographical Dictionaries Master Index: A Consolidated Index to Biographical Information concerning Historical Personages in Over 35 of the Principal Retrospective Biographical Dictionaries.* Detroit, MI: Gale, 1980.

Contains citations to biographical information for more than 304,000 entries. Entries include name, life dates, and codes for the sources for the biographies. Full bibliographical information is supplied for each source.

135. Silverman, Judith. *Index to Collective Biographies for Young Readers: Elementary and Junior High School Level.* 3d ed. New York: R. R. Bowker, 1979.

More than 7,000 individuals who appear in over 900 collective biographies are listed in this index. Silverman also indicates which of the books were out of print when the index was compiled.

136. *New York Times Biographical Service.* Ann Arbor, MI: University Microfilm International, 1974–. Monthly.

Reprints biographical articles published in the *New York Times.* Published monthly with an index to the service printed in December of each year.

137. Filby, P. William, and Meyer, Mary K. *Passenger and Immigration Lists Index: A Guide to Published Arrival Records of About 500,000 Passengers Who Came to the United States and Canada in the Seventeenth, Eighteenth and Nineteenth Centuries.* 3 volumes plus supplements in 1982, 1983, 1984. Detroit, MI: Gale, 1981.

This work indexes North and South American immigration and ship passenger lists. Each entry includes the male immigrant's name, his age, port of entry and date, an accession number for the list indexed, and page number. If a wife or children were listed with the husband or father entering, their names appear with his entry. Cross-references provide access to these women's and children's names.

The index includes immigrants entering South American or Canadian ports, but the emphasis is on those entering the United States. The original *Index* was published in 1981 with supplements appearing regularly.

138. Falk, Byron A., Jr., and Falk, Valerie R. *Personal Name Index to the New York Times Index 1851–1974.* 22 volumes. Succasunna, NJ: Roxbury Data Interface, 1976–.

An index to individual names appearing in the *New York Times Index* for the years 1851–1974. Living persons as well as death notices are included. References are to the *Index* volume and page numbers. The index is not yet complete; volumes cover the alphabet through the letter S. A supplement, beginning with volume 23, 1975/79, began publication in 1979.

II. Historical Sources

139. Horan, James D. *The Authentic Wild West: The Gunfighters.* New York: Crown, 1976.

> An introduction is followed by lengthy biographical essays on individual gunfighters and their times. Notes and a bibliography are included.

140. ———. *The Authentic Wild West: The Lawmen.* New York: Crown, 1980.

> An introductory essay on the frontier of the lawmen, with photographs and facsimiles of clippings. The essay is followed by individual biographical sketches on major lawmen and women who interested them. Notes and a bibliography are included.

141. ———. *The Authentic Wild West: The Outlaws.* New York: Crown, 1976.

> An introductory essay is followed by individual biographical essays on outlaws of the period. Notes and a bibliography are included.

142. Herwig, Holger H., and Heyman, Neil M. *Biographical Dictionary of World War I.* Westport, CT: Greenwood Press, 1982.

> This is a source of biographical information on the chief participants of World War I. Six essay chapters discussing facets of the war begin this reference work. The dictionary section contains entries giving the individual's name, country and rank (e.g., Rumania, King), family background, and a discussion of the subject's life. Sources of biographical information are cited in the entries. The biographical narratives are interesting summaries of large amounts of biographical data. Appendices include a chronology and a listing of the biographees by their principal occupations. There is also a 12-page bibliography.

143. Tunney, Christopher. *A Biographical Dictionary of World War II.* New York: St. Martin's Press, 1972.

> Contains sketches on military and political figures, journalists, and artists who are remembered for their roles during the Second World War. All nationalities are represented.

144. Franklin, Benjamin V. *Boston Printers, Publishers, and Booksellers: 1640–1800.* Boston: G.K. Hall, 1980.

> Covered are the first 1½ centuries of printing and publishing. Name and title indices provide additional access to the entries, which contain biographical data, listings of authors and works the individual was responsible for printing or publishing, and business relationships.

145. Uden, Grant, and Cooper, Richard. *A Dictionary of British Ships and Seamen*. New York: St. Martin's, 1981.

In addition to biographies of British seafarers and naval heroes, *A Dictionary of British Ships and Seamen* contains sketches on ships, famous ports, battles, shipping and sailing jargon, and seafaring lore. Most biographies are of famous British sea captains, but there are exceptions. Monarchs, such as King Edward III and Queen Elizabeth I, who are known for their support of sea exploration and the British Navy, have brief entries. Author Joseph Conrad is included for the body of literature he produced with nautical themes and settings. Geographer and cartographer Sebastian Cabot appears for his contribution to exploration.

The alphabetically arranged sketches are short, emphasizing the subject's sea career, not his private life. Appendices provide maps, schematic drawings of ships, and other information.

146. Davis, Burke. *Heroes of the American Revolution*. New York: Random House, 1971.

Eleven prominent patriots are profiled in this illustrated book. [Juvenile]

147. Bakeless, John, and Bakeless, Katherine. *Signers of the Declaration*. Boston: Houghton Mifflin, 1969.

Contains biographies of the men who signed the Declaration of Independence, arranged by the colony each represented. Each entry includes a reproduction of the subject's signature and stresses the events that led to that person's participation as a delegate to the Continental Congress, as well as his political life during and after the Revolutionary War.

148. Keegan, John. *Who Was Who in World War II*. London: Arms and Armour Press, 1978.

A heavily illustrated guide to the major political and military figures of the Second World War.

III. Regional Sources

149. *Biographical Directory of the South Carolina House of Representatives.* 3 volumes to date. Columbia, SC: University of South Carolina Press, 1974, 1977, 1981.

> Volume 1 contains Session lists for each meeting of the Assembly from 1692 to 1973. The other 2 volumes contain biographical sketches of those individuals for 1692–1775 and 1775–90 respectively.

150. *Biographical Souvenir of the States of Georgia and Florida: Containing Biographical Sketches of the Representative Public, and Many Early Settled Families in These States.* Chicago: F. A. Battey, 1889. Reprint. Easley, SC: Southern Historical Press, n.d.

> An illustrated guide to the nineteenth-century luminaries of these 2 southern states. Most of the entries feature persons living in 1889, but some recently deceased individuals are included as well.

151. Coleman, Kenneth, and Gurr, Charles Stephen. *Dictionary of Georgia Biography.* 2 volumes. Athens, GA: University of Georgia Press, 1983.

> In their preface, the editors state that "The primary criterion for inclusion in the *Dictionary* was that the subject has done something of statewide significance while a resident in Georgia." The signed entries are approximately one page in length, and they include a short bibliography of additional readings.

152. Knight, Lucian Lamar. *Encyclopedia of Georgia Biography.* Atlanta, GA: A. H. Cawston, 1931.

> Biographies of selected famous Georgians, from the founding of the state through the early 1930s. Portraits accompany most entries.

153. Coleman, Kenneth, and Erney, Jackie. *Famous Georgians.* Atlanta, GA: Georgia Department of Archives and History, 1976.

> Published in honor of the National Bicentennial Celebration, this slim volume contains portraits of 29 individuals who influenced Georgia history or brought fame to the Peach State. A bibliography is included.

154. Montgomery, Horace. *Georgians in Profile: Historical Essays in Honor of Ellis Merton Coulter.* Athens, GA: University of Georgia Press, 1958.

> Essays on 14 individuals who contributed to the founding, development, and growth of Georgia.

155. Miller, Zell. *Great Georgians.* Franklin Springs, GA: Advocate Press, 1983.
> Biographical profiles of 47 Georgians, published in honor of the 250th anniversary of the founding of the colony by Sir James Edward Oglethorpe. Arranged alphabetically, each entry includes a portrait.

156. *History of Georgia*, 4 volumes. Chicago: S. J. Clarke Pub. Co., 1926.
> The final 3 volumes of this set contain biographies, many with portraits, of the influential Georgians who were mentioned in Volume I. All 4 volumes are heavily illustrated. Written by then editor of the *Atlanta Constitution* Clark Howell, Volume I of this series relates the history of Georgia from "the earliest period of historical records of the aboriginal life" to 1925.

157. Northen, William J. *Men of Mark in Georgia: A Complete and Elaborate History of the State from Its Settlement to the Present Time, Chiefly Told in Biographies and Autobiographies of the Most Eminent Men of Each Period of Georgia's Progress and Development.* 7 volumes. Atlanta, GA: A. B. Caldwell, 1906, 1908, 1910, 1912. Reprint. Spartanburg, SC: The Reprint Co., 1974.
> Covering the years 1733–1911, *Men of Mark in Georgia* contains short signed and illustrated biographies of famous Georgians, from the colonial founders through the early twentieth century.

158. *Personalities of the South.* 10th ed. Raleigh, NC: American Biographical Institute, 1979.
> Covered in this volume are prominent individuals from Alabama, Arkansas, Florida, Georgia, Kentucky, Louisiana, Maryland, Mississippi, North Carolina, Oklahoma, Puerto Rico, South Carolina, Tennessee, Texas, Virginia, the Virgin Islands, and West Virginia. A state-by-state listing of names appears at the end of the book.

159. *Who's Who in Georgia.* Atlanta, GA: Southern Highlands Foundation, 1982.
> A directory of "outstanding citizens of the State of Georgia."

160. Crawford, Geddings Hardy. *Who's Who in South Carolina: A Dictionary of Contemporaries Containing Biographical Notices of Eminent Men of South Carolina.* Columbia, SC: McCaw of Columbia, 1921.
> A dictionary of prominent South Carolinians living in the early 1920s.

161. *Who's Who in the East.* Chicago: Marquis Who's Who. Biannual.
> A *Who's Who* publication listing over 19,000 individuals from Connecticut, Delaware, Maine, New Hampshire, New Jersey, New York, Pennsylvania, Rhode Island, Vermont, and Washington, DC, in the U.S. and the Canadian provinces of New Brunswick, Newfoundland, Nova Scotia, Prince Edward Island, Quebec, and eastern Ontario. Regional importance is emphasized to eliminate duplication with names in *Who's Who in America*, although some individuals appear in both.

162. *Who's Who in the Midwest.* Chicago: Marquis Who's Who.
Biannual.
   This work contains 21,000 names of men and women of distinction in
   the midwestern region of the United States including Illinois, Indiana,
   Iowa, Kansas, Michigan, Minnesota, Missouri, Nebraska, North Dakota,
   Ohio, South Dakota, and Wisconsin, and in Canada the provinces of
   Manitoba and western Ontario. Biographical sketches are arranged al-
   phabetically by name, 3 columns to the page.

163. *Who's Who in the West.* Chicago: Marquis Who's Who.
Biannual.
   Includes individuals from the states of Alaska, Arizona, California, Colo-
   rado, Hawaii, Idaho, Montana, Nevada, New Mexico, Oregon, Utah,
   Washington, and Wyoming, and the Canadian provinces of Alberta,
   British Columbia, and Saskatchewan.

163a. *Who's Who in the South and Southwest.* Chicago: Marquis
Who's Who. Biannual.
   Over 19,000 prominent residents of the burgeoning sunbelt are profiled
   in this regional dictionary. States included are Alabama, Arkansas, Flor-
   ida, Georgia, Kentucky, Louisiana, Mississippi, North Carolina, South
   Carolina, Oklahoma, Tennessee, Texas, Virginia, and West Virginia.
   Puerto Rico, the Virgin Islands, and Mexico are also included.

IV. The Military

164. Spiller, Roger J.; Dawson, Joseph G., III; and Williams, T. Harry. *Dictionary of American Military Biography.* 3 volumes. Westport, CT: Greenwood Press, 1984.

> Biographies of American military leaders from the colonial era to the present comprise this work. Essays run from a paragraph to several pages in length, and a short bibliography concludes each signed entry. Appendices include a chronology of American military developments, lists of American military ranks and units, an index of persons by birthplace, and 2 other indexes: entries by conflict and by service. An overall index of names and places concludes the final volume.

165. Johnston, Charles H. L. *Famous Cavalry Leaders Through the Ages with the Heroes of Sabre, Spur, and Saddle; with Faithful Accounts of their Forced Marches, Dashing Raids, and Glorious Charges.* Boston: L. C. Page and Company, 1908.

> Fifteen cavalry leaders are glorified in narratives relating their great deeds in battle. Some of the individuals listed include Attila the Hun, Genghis Khan, Chevalier Bayard, Gustavus Adolphus, Francis Marion, Marshall Ney, Jeb Stuart, and George Armstrong Custer.

166. Warner, Ezra J. *Generals in Blue: Lives of the Union Commanders.* Baton Rouge, LA: Louisiana State University Press, 1964.

> A companion volume to the 1959 title *Generals in Gray*, this volume traces the military careers of those men who led the Union troops to victory in the American Civil War. Cross-references help the reader link friends, rivals, and contemporaries. Not limited only to generals, the sketches include portraits whenever possible. Appendices give brevet ranks, state of birth, and a list of campaigns and battles. There is no index, but an extensive footnotes and bibliography section will assist any Civil War researcher in pursuit of additional information.

167. ———. *Generals in Gray: Lives of the Confederate Commanders.* Baton Rouge, LA: Louisiana State University Press, 1959.

> Biographical sketches of the general officers of the Confederate forces. Most entries include a portrait, and there is a lengthy bibliography at the end of the book.

168. Schuon, Karl. *U.S. Navy Biographical Dictionary.* New York: Franklin Watts, Inc., 1964.

Biographical sketches of "the giants of naval warfare," as well as most Navy Medal of Honor winners. The appendix lists the Secretaries of the Navy from Benjamin Stoddard (1798–1801) to Paul Henry Nitze, who commenced his duty in 1963.

169. Carver, Sir Michael, Field-Marshal. *The War Lords: Military Commanders of the Twentieth Century.* Boston: Little, Brown, 1976.

Chapter-length biographies of 43 twentieth-century military leaders, largely from the First and Second World Wars. Coverage is international, although British and American commanders dominate the roster of entries. Biographees includes only those men who commanded a "considerable force" of fighters in an important campaign. Excluded were those who fought in the Russo-Japanese and Sino-Japanese conflicts and men who have earned their reputations fighting guerrilla and terrorist warfare.

170. *Webster's American Military Biographies.* Springfield, MA: G. & C. Merriam, 1978. Reprint. New York: Dover, 1984.

An alphabetical guide to the careers of 1,033 Americans who served in the military. Both living and dead persons are included, and coverage is current through the Vietnam conflict. Addenda include chronological lists of military commanders and a chronology of battles, listing which men commanded the forces at each event.

171. *Who Was Who in American History: The Military.* Chicago: Marquis Who's Who, 1975.

Brief biographical sketches of 10,000 deceased military leaders from the years 1607–1972.

172. Keegan, John, and Wheatcroft, Andrew. *Who's Who in Military History: From 1453 to the Present Day.* New York: William Morrow & Co., Inc., 1976.

An illustrated biographical dictionary of military leaders of the modern era: from the "age of firearms," which began in 1453, to the time of publication. Coverage is international and portraits accompany the short sketches. A glossary of military terms and continental maps showing battle sites conclude the work.

173. Martell, Paul, and Hayes, Grace P. *World Military Leaders.* New York: R. R. Bowker, 1975.

Covers senior military and civilian personnel in military establishments worldwide. One section lists the biographies in alphabetical order; the second section lists them by country served. Emphasis is on military-related careers.

V. The World of Government and Politics

GENERAL

174. Barone, Michael, and Ujifusa, Grant. *The Almanac of American Politics 1986: The President, the Senators, the Representatives, the Governors: Their Records and Election Results, Their States and Districts.* Washington, DC: National Journal, Inc., 1984. Annual.

Arrangement is alphabetical by state. Within these state sections are profiles of the governor, senators, and representatives, arranged by district. Background material is provided for each state, and each biographical sketch includes congressional rating statistics, key votes, election results, campaign expenditures, and contributions.

Special features include "Congress and Governors at a Glance," an alphabetical listing of the members of Congress and each of the governors, with references to the page numbers on which their biographies appear. "Districts at a Glance" is a guide to the geographic area represented by each member of Congress. There is a handy guide to usage, a list of abbreviations, and a series of background articles, all designed to acquaint the user with the executive and legislative branches of the federal government and the demographics of the nation they represent.

Photographs are included for each of the biographies. Additional background articles cover campaign finance and Senate and House committees. There is a subject index.

175. Reincke, Mary, and Lichterman, Nancy. *The American Bench: Judges of the Nation.* 2d ed. Minneapolis, MN: Reginald Bishop Forster & Associates, Inc., 1978. (See also *American Political Women: Contemporary and Historical Profiles.*)

Approximately 15,000 judges at all levels of federal and state courts are included. Grouping is by state and jurisdiction. A name index is provided as a finding aid. Jurisdictional maps are also included.

176. Kallenbach, Joseph E., and Kallenbach, Jessamine S. *American State Governors, 1776–1976.* 3 volumes. Dobbs Ferry, NY: Oceana Publications, Inc., 1982.

An invaluable source tracing the history of each state's governorship from its earliest federal beginnings to the mid-1970s. Volume 1 contains electoral and personal data; volumes 2 and 3 contain the biographical essays, arranged chronologically within each state. A list of sources and a cumulative index conclude the third volume.

177. Parker, Thomas. *America's Foreign Policy 1945–1976: Its Creators and Critics.* New York: Facts on File, 1980.

Provides sketches of 63 selected political figures in American foreign policy from the end of World War II to the election of Jimmy Carter. Two criteria merit inclusion in the work: presidential influence or distinction in the field of political analysis. Those with presidential influence include individuals whose advice was taken seriously by an administration, though not necessarily heeded, as well as those who represented the majority of political thought among Americans. Thus presidents, ambassadors, advisors, academicians, journalists, scientists, military personnel, and also-rans appear on these pages. A lengthy introduction describes the important issues of the period. Also included is a calendar of dates and events of the period and bibliographic essays on each of the presidential administrations covered.

178. *Attorneys General of the United States, 1789–1979.* Washington, DC: U.S. Government Printing Office, 1980.

Brief biographical information accompanies the portraits of 70 U.S. attorneys general.

179. Lanman, Charles. *Biographical Annals of the Civil Government of the United States during its First Century.* Washington, DC: James Anglim, 1876.

Sketches of the "Delegates to the Colonial and Continental Congresses, the Senators, Representatives and Territorial Delegates of the Federal Congress, Cabinet Ministers, Justices of the Supreme and other Federal Courts, officials of the Executive Departments, Governors of States and Territories, Diplomatic Ministers," and others who served in government through 1875. A "Tabular Records" section provides lists of delegates, congressional sessions, cabinet members, military leaders, etc. A general index at the close of the book provides access by names of all entries.

180. Holli, Melvin G., and Jones, Peter d'A. *Biographical Dictionary of American Mayors, 1820–1980: Big City Mayors.* Westport, CT: Greenwood Press, 1981.

The editor selected 15 cities which since 1820 have been leaders in population and historical importance. The biographical narratives are in alphabetical order and include bibliographical sources. Appendices include chronological lists of mayors by city, party affiliation, ethnic background, religion, and place of birth. There are also appendices on the population increase/decrease of the cities and analyses of the population ethnicity.

181. Burkholder, Mark A., and Chandler, D. S. *Biographical Dictionary of Audencia Ministers in the Americas, 1687–1821.* Westport, CT: Greenwood Press, 1982.

Biographies of the men who served as judges or Crown attorneys in the colonial Spanish "audencias," or regional courts of appeal. These men were highly educated and had great influence with the colonial executives. Entries trace each man's rise to his appointment to the Audencia and provide a list of sources (usually archival materials) from which the information was derived.

182. Kuehl, Warren F. *Biographical Dictionary of Internationalists.* Westport, CT: Greenwood Press, 1983.
For the purposes of this reference work, "Internationalists" refers to those people who advocate world organization. Coverage is of deceased advocates and ranges from 1800 to the present. Entries include biographical data but also include the individual's activities, ideas, and contributions as Internationalists. Appendices provide access to individuals by country of birth, career, and interests.

183. Chase, Harold, et al. *Biographical Dictionary of the Federal Judiciary.* Detroit, MI: Gale Research Co., 1976.
Profiled here are U.S. federal judges serving with lifetime tenure anytime during the years 1789–1974. Judges who were listed in *Who's Who* or *Who Was Who* are represented here by reproductions of those biographies. For other judges, other biographical sources were consulted. Judges from the following courts are included: the Supreme Court, 1789–1974; the United States Courts of Appeal, 1801–02 (now called Circuit Court, 1891–1974); the United States District Courts, 1789–1974; the United States Court of Claims, 1855–1974; the United States Court of Customs and Patent Appeals, 1909–74; the United States Customs Court, 1926–74; the Commerce Court (now defunct), 1910–13; and the Supreme Court of the District of Columbia (now the United States District Court for the District of Columbia), 1863–1936. Facts about these judges are listed in brief alphabetical form. Numerous tables indicate their religious preferences, political parties, political offices, and occupations.

184. Raimo, John W. *Biographical Directory of American Colonial and Revolutionary Governors, 1607–1789.* Westport, CT: Meckler Books, 1980.
Biographies are listed chronologically within colonies. The usual biographical data for the 400 people included are provided; bibliographies are integral to the entries. Not all biographees held the title of "governor," but all functioned in the equivalent position. Many relatively obscure officeholders are included.

185. Kennedy, Lawrence F. *Biographical Directory of the American Congress 1774–1971.* 11th ed. Washington, DC: U.S. Government Printing Office, 1971.
Included in this work are more than 10,800 biographies. In addition, this volume includes biographies of U.S. presidents who never served in Congress. Contents include listings of executive officers during the years 1789–1971, the Continental Congress with names and dates of members arranged by state, and a table showing representatives under each apportionment from the Continental Congress through the 19th Census in 1970. Another section is composed of a series of listings of members of Congress arranged by state, beginning with the first Congress and ending with the members of the 91st Congress, 1969–71.

186. Sobel, Robert, and Raimo, John. *Biographical Directory of the Governors of the United States, 1789–1978.* 4 volumes. Westport, CT: Meckler Books, 1978.

The directory includes biographies of approximately 2,000 men and women who served as state governors between 1789 and 1978. The arrangement is alphabetical by state, beginning with Alabama in volume 1 and ending with Wyoming in volume 4. Within each state, the listing is chronological. There is an informative introduction which discusses the office of governor as it has evolved over the years. At the end of each volume is an alphabetical listing of governors with a reference to the volume and page number where each biography appears.

187. *Biographical Directory of the Senate of the State of South Carolina 1776–1964.* Columbia, SC: South Carolina Archives Department, 1964.

Compiled by the Senatorial Research Committee, this is a list of representatives to the Senate by district, followed by an alphabetical biographical directory on those individuals.

188. Sobel, Robert. *Biographical Directory of the United States Executive Branch, 1774–1971.* Westport, CT: Greenwood Publishing Co., 1971.

This volume contains alphabetically arranged career biographies of all United States Cabinet heads, presidents, vice presidents, and presidents of the Continental Congress. It is intended as a single source for the little-known as well as the famous. Each biography includes major accomplishments, significant dates, family affiliation, and service prior to and following Cabinet duty. In addition, each biography includes bibliographical references to primary and secondary works which provide further information. There are nearly 500 biographies included which are accessible by a name index and a series of special indices which cover presidential administrations; heads of state and Cabinet officials; other federal government service, state, county, and municipal government service; military service by branch; education; place of birth; and marital information.

189. *Congressional Directory.* See *Official Congressional Directory* (200).

190. *Congressional Quarterly's Guide to the U. S. Supreme Court.* Washington, DC: Congressional Quarterly, Inc., 1979.

Part 6 of this encyclopedic history of the highest court in the United States is a biographical guide to its justices.

191. *Countries of the World and their Leaders Yearbook.* 2 volumes. Detroit, MI: Gale, 1985.

Preceding the general information on the various nations is a section on the leaders of these countries. A listing of officials in the countries is also included.

192. *Directory of Registered Lobbyists and Lobbyist Legislation.* 2d ed. Chicago: Marquis Academic Media, 1975.

A directory of state and federal registered lobbyists. The book includes the laws for each state regarding who may register as a lobbyist and how the lobbyist may pursue his/her task. Following is a state-by-state list of lobbyists and the organizations they represent. An organization index provides cross-references to all lobbyists representing a particular interest group. No biographical information is included with the entries for lobbyists.

193. Cook, James F. *Governors of Georgia.* Huntsville, AL: The Strode Publishers, Inc., 1979.

Arranged chronologically, this book profiles the men who served as governor of Georgia, from John Reynolds, the colony's first royal governor, to George D. Busbee, who served from 1975 to 1983. Portraits and photographs accompany most sketches. There is a bibliography at the end of the book.

194. Solomon, Samuel R. *The Governors of the American States, Commonwealths, and Territories, 1900–1980.* Lexington, KY: Council of State Governments, 1980.

Governors are listed chronologically by administration within each state. Brief biographical data are provided. Also included is a brief bibliography on governors.

195. *Guide to the U.S. Supreme Court.* See *Congressional Quarterly's Guide to the U.S. Supreme Court* (190).

196. Bicentennial Committee of the Judicial Conference of the United States. *Judges of the United States.* 2d ed. Washington, DC: U.S. Government Printing Office, 1983.

A guide to all individuals who have served as federal court judges. Arranged alphabetically, the book includes 3 indices: one by appointing president, one by year of appointment, and a name index.

197. Barnes, Catherine A. *Men of the Supreme Court: Profiles of the Justices.* New York: Facts on File, 1978.

Justices appointed from 1925 to 1975 appear in this volume. Entries include vital information, previous positions in government, tenure on the Court, and educational background. The text of each entry traces the justices' political philosophy, as well as their judicial behavior over time. Notable cases earn the most scrutiny, and the author provides ample references to significant cases. A detailed preface provides a history of the Supreme Court from 1945 to the mid–70s. Profiles appear alphabetically. A chronology of court appointments from 1925–75 shows retirements and deaths as well as appointments. Significant decisions that took place during the years 1945–76 are listed, and an extensive bibliographic essay precedes a traditional bibliography and indices of cases and names.

198. Camp, Roderic A. *Mexican Political Biographies 1935–1981.* 2d ed., revised and expanded. Tucson, AZ: University of Arizona Press, 1982.

In his "Note to the Reader," Camp writes: "This volume contains the biographies of public men, living or deceased, who have been prominent in Mexican political life from 1935 to mid 1980." In addition to providing brief sketches on these figures, Camp indexed their entries in several other historical and biographical sources on Mexico.

Appendices list chronologically those persons holding major elective and appointive offices at the federal and state levels. Those profiled in the text appear in italics. A lengthy bibliographic essay completes the work.

199. Pickrill, D. A. *Ministers of the Crown.* Boston: Routledge & Kegan Paul, 1981.
Holders of ministerial posts in the United Kingdom are listed from the earliest possible date. The chronological listing by office indicates the minister's name and his tenure in office.

200. U.S. Congress. *Official Congressional Directory.* Washington, DC: U.S. Government Printing Office. Issued by each elected Congress.
Despite the limited coverage implied by its title, the *Official Congressional Directory* provides biographical and directory information on the Cabinet; the judicial branch; and semi-independent agency directors, ambassadors, and other federal employees of rank in addition to members of Congress.
The biographical section of the *Directory* lists states alphabetically. Senators lead the entry, with senior senators appearing first. Members of Congress are listed numerically by district, and each district's geographic contents are listed. Information in the sketches focuses on the congressperson's background and political career.
An index of names at the back provides access to the profiles, as well as to committee appointments, agency rosters, etc. The table of contents serves as a subject index.

201. Schoenebaum, Eleanora V. *Political Profiles.* 5 volumes. New York: Facts on File, 1978–.
Scheduled to include 6 volumes so that 3 decades of post-World War II presidencies are covered, the *Political Profiles* series features biographies of political figures prominent in each administration. Although government officeholders predominate, journalists and well-known political activists (such as William F. Buckley and Jane Fonda) appear on these pages as well. Biographies focus on the individual's contributions during the volume's years of coverage. Consequently, some individuals appear in several volumes, with different information given each time.
Appendices include a chronology of administration highlights, a list of congressional members for the period covered, and a lengthy bibliography. There is an index.
The 5 volumes completed thus far are: volume 1, *The Truman Years*; volume 2, *The Eisenhower Years*; volume 3, *The Kennedy Years*; volume 4, *The Johnson Years*; and volume 5, *The Nixon/Ford Years.*

202. Ehrenhalt, Alan, and Healy, Robert E. *Politics in America: Members of Congress in Washington and at Home 1984.* Washington, DC: Congressional Quarterly Press, 1983. Biannual.
Lists members of Congress, grouped by state, with biographical sketches of each, plus voting patterns, election results, and information on campaign finances.

203. Acheson, Dean. *Present at the Creation: My Years in the State Department.* New York: W. W. Norton & Co., Inc., 1969.
This volume of the memoirs of one of this century's most famous secretaries of state is not a true biographical source. Nevertheless, Ach-

eson's 11 years in the State Department (from 1941–52) exposed him to the most powerful people in the world during a crucial time in modern history. Acheson's highly detailed index provides access to his comments and thoughts about most of these influential figures, thus rendering the book invaluable to students of mid-twentieth-century history. Portraits of many of these famous people appear in an insert.

204. Lippmann, Walter, and Harrison, Gilbert A. *Public Persons.* New York: Liveright, 1976.

A collection of 48 essays written by Lippmann over the course of his career. The essays were part of the Lippmann collection of Yale University's Sterling Library. The essays are partly biographical, but they also reflect Lippmann's political philosophy. Each is dated, and editor Harrison concludes each one with a postscript about the subject's relationship to Lippmann or his work.

205. Rose, Martha, et al. *Rulers and Governments of the World.* 3 volumes. New York: R. R. Bowker, 1978.

Each volume covers a particular time span: volume 1, earliest times to 1491; volume 2, 1492–1929; and volume 3, 1930–1975.

Rulers are grouped within territories, ecclesiastical sees, dynasties, peoples, and hordes. For each ruler, date of attaining power is given. Date of birth is given if known as is kinship to preceding ruler. The death date is given if it differs from the reign's end. An index helps in locating divisions not easily identified. A bibliography is included. There is an index of persons.

206. Millichamp, Josephine. *Senators from Georgia.* Huntsville, AL: The Strode Publishers, Inc., 1976.

Biographical sketches on the 53 men who served as Georgia's representatives to the United States Senate anytime during the years 1789–1976. A short bibliography and index are included, as are illustrations.

207. *State Elective Officials and the Legislatures 1985–86.* Lexington, KY: Council of State Governments, 1985. Annual.

This is supplement one to the *Book of the States.* The supplement is an annual directory of the members of the legislatures of all 50 states, plus 5 American territories: American Samoa, Guam, Northern Mariana Islands, Puerto Rico, and the Virgin Islands.

208. *State Legislative Leadership, Committees and Staff 1985–86.* Lexington, KY: Council of State Governments, 1985. Annual.

An annual directory of the legislative leaders, and committee chairpersons in the 50 states and 5 U.S. territories. Entries are listed alphabetically by state, then cross-listed by title in this second supplement to the *Book of the States.*

209. Morris, Dan, and Morris, Inez. *Who Was Who in American Politics: A Biographical Dictionary of Over 4,000 Men and Women Who Contributed to the United States Political Scene from Colonial Days up to and Including the Immediate Past.* New York: Hawthorn Books, 1974.

The authors' note describes this volume as "a biographical dictionary of past political figures, most of them dead, others of them still alive but (to the best of our knowledge) no longer active on the national political scene."

210. *Who's Who in American Politics, 1981–1982.* 8th ed. New York: R. R. Bowker, 1981.

Twenty-two thousand politically active people are included at many levels within each state. Preliminary pages list the president and members of the Cabinet, the state delegations, state governors, and state party chairpersons. Biographical vitae of politically active individuals are in brief listing form and are grouped alphabetically within states. Information supplied includes education, vocation, positions held, memberships, religion, and address.

THE U.S. PRESIDENCY

211. Whitney, David C. *The American Presidents.* New York: Doubleday, 1978.

Biographical sketches are included on the administrations of presidents in office from Washington through Carter. Also included are collections of key facts about the officeholders, historical sites relevant to the presidents, and comments the ex-presidents have made about the office.

212. Quinn, Sandra L., and Kanter, Sanford. *America's Royalty: All the Presidents' Children.* Westport, CT: Greenwood Press, 1983.

Coverage is through the Reagan administration and includes both legitimate and known illegitimate children of presidents. Children are listed by birth order within their father's term(s) of office. Basic biographical data are included followed by a brief biographical sketch. Each presidential family concludes with a bibliography. In the appendix are listed tables of schools attended, occupations of the children, native state, longevity, and cause of death for each president. A personal name index is also provided.

213. Williamson, David, and Burke's Peerage. *Burke's Presidential Families of the United States of America.* London: Burke's Peerage Ltd., 1975.

This work traces the lineage of American presidents through Gerald Ford. Each entry includes a brief narrative sketch, portraits, a chronology, a list of writings, and a statement of lineage. The body of the entry is taken up by an exhaustive list of the president's descendants. At the end of the list of descendants are included any brothers or sisters. The biographies were all written by Marcus and Lesley Hume Cunliffe; a background essay on the presidency of the United States was written by Dennis Brogan.

214. DeGregorio, William A. *The Complete Book of U.S. Presidents.* New York: Dembner Books, 1984; distributed by W. W. Norton.

This is not only a factual reference aid but an entertaining book to read. The presidents—all 39 of them—have been interesting characters for the most part, although some are better known than others. Each has a chapter of his own in which the usual biographical information is intertwined with personality, marital (and extramarital) data; physical description; adolescence; presidential career; and other information.

215. Kane, Joseph Nathan. *Facts about the Presidents: A Compilation of Biographical and Historical Information.* 4th ed. New York: H. W. Wilson, 1981.
This classic biographical reference work has been updated through the Reagan administration. Substantive as well as trivial information is included.

216. Feerick, John D., and Feerick, Emalie P. *The First Book of Vice-Presidents of the United States.* 7th rev. ed. New York: Franklin Watts, 1981.
This slim reference work includes vice-presidents through George Bush. An introductory essay discusses the office itself. Interesting in style, this source is informative about often forgotten holders of this office.

217. Klapthor, Margaret Brown. *The First Ladies.* Washington, DC: U.S. Government Printing Office, 1981.
This slight reference book includes brief biographical sketches of each first lady through Nancy Reagan; each sketch is accompanied by portraits.

218. Young, Klyde, and Middleton, Lamar. *Heirs Apparent: The Vice Presidents of the United States.* New York: Prentice-Hall, 1948.
The 34 vice-presidents through Harry S. Truman are covered. Ten actually became presidents themselves.

219. Clark, Mary Fairman. *Lives of the Presidents of the United States.* Boston: DeWolfe, Fiske & Co., n.d.
This illustrated volume contains children's-level biographies of the first 25 chief executives. [Juvenile]

220. Freidel, Frank. *Our Country's Presidents.* Washington, DC: National Geographic Society, 1966.
Lives of the presidents, originally appearing in the *National Geographic,* are collected in 5 chapters, covering presidents through Lyndon Johnson. The chapter groupings reflect periods of American history, such as the Western Movement or the Atomic Age.

221. Armbruster, Maxim Ethan. *The President of the United States: A New Appraisal from Washington to Kennedy.* Rev. and expanded, 1963. New York: Horizon Press, 1982.
Profiles of the chief executives through the 35th president. The well-written chapters emphasize unique qualities in each president, as well as highlights and low points of his administration. Each entry includes election results from all victorious campaigns. Portraits of each chief executive appear at the beginning of the book. A bibliography and index offer access to additional names and information sources.

222. Southwick, Leslie H. *Presidential Also–Rans and Running Mates, 1788-1980.* Jefferson, NC: McFarland, 1984.
How soon we forget those people we read about in history classes who aspired to the highest offices in the land but never made it! The

arrangement is chronological; the writing is interesting; the facts are correct. Each candidate's background, qualifications, offices held, and other data are included in an entry along with a bibliography in each section.

223. Graff, Henry F. *The Presidents: A Reference History.* New York: Scribner's, 1984.

Thirty-three essays profile the men who occupied the United States Presidency through Jimmy Carter. Curiously, Theodore Roosevelt and William Howard Taft are excluded. Arranged chronologically, each chapter-length essay provides biographical data as well as an analysis of the administration. Annotated bibliographies of additional works are included.

224. Beard, William. *The Presidents in American History: Brought Forward Since 1948.* New York: Julian Messner, Inc., 1981.

Brief biographical chapters describe the presidencies of chief executives from Washington through Eisenhower. Portraits accompany each sketch. The most valuable portion of the book is "The Biographical Digest" which appears at the end. It includes birth, marriage, and death dates; a brief résumé of each man's career; the dates of his term of office; and the names of his vice-presidents and Cabinet members. Election results, including opposing candidates and popular and electoral votes, are also included.

225. Armbruster, Maxim E. *Presidents of the United States and Their Administrations from Washington to Reagan.* 7th rev. ed. New York: Horizon Press, 1983.

Each profile is preceded by a breakdown of the final vote count for each election. The profiles themselves are descriptive and analytical, detailing influences on the presidents' careers and their major contributions.

226. Freidel, Frank Burt. *Presidents of the United States of America.* 9th ed. Washington, DC: White House Historical Association, 1982.

This slim paperbound volume is intended to be a souvenir item for visitors to Washington, DC, and the White House. One-page biographical sketches of each president from Washington to Reagan are accompanied by portraits of each chief executive.

227. Bassett, Margaret. *Profiles and Portraits of American Presidents.* New York: David McKay, 1976.

Coverage is through 1975 when Gerald Ford was in office; thus 38 presidents are included in narratives.

228. Stone, Irving. *They Also Ran: The Story of the Men Who Were Defeated for the Presidency.* Garden City, NY: Doubleday, Doran and Co., Inc., 1966.

Organized into "books" that tie defeated candidates together by type, this volume takes a unique approach to a well-worn topic: the U.S. presidency. Rather than profiling these highly visible but quickly forgotten losers chronologically, Stone has grouped them by profession, so that journalists Horace Greeley (1872) and James Middleton Cox (1920) appear together, as do lawyers John W. Davis (1924) and Wendell L.

Willkie (1940). The epilog includes a list of candidates by party and year, indicating a victory or loss. A bibliography and index conclude the work.

229. Vexler, Robert I. *Vice-Presidents and Cabinet Members: Biographies Arranged Chronologically by Administration.* 2 volumes. Dobbs Ferry, NY: Oceana Publications, Inc., 1975.

As the title indicates, this work offers profiles of those who served in presidential administrations from George Washington to Gerald Ford. Sketches focus on the political careers of those profiled, and each concludes with a short bibliography of sources.

VI. Royalty and Important Families

230. Shepherd, Jack. *The Adams Chronicles: Four Generations of Greatness*. Boston: Little, Brown, 1975.

A history of the Adams family, from John and Abigail to their great grandchildren. Beautifully illustrated, the book relies heavily on the Adams correspondence to flesh out these historically prominent characters.

231. Townsend, Peter. *Burke's Genealogical and Heraldic History of the Peerage, Baronetage, and Knightage*. 105th ed. London: Burke's Peerage, 1975.

The Burke's publications indicate Great Britain's holders of hereditary titles and provide genealogical guides to that person's lineage. Thus, one may trace a title from its first holder to the present. Peers, barons, and knights of the realm are listed in Burke's, as are successions and extensions of peerages and baronetcies. Newly created life peerages are also included. Each biographical entry begins with the surname and its crest. The current titleholder is profiled first with his educational background, other titles, degrees, posts, war honors, and offspring. Below that is the man's lineage, starting with the title's first holder, and including the title's dates of creation, advancement, and succession. A description of the arms follows, and addresses are provided for the district represented in the House of Lords, as well as the "town [London] residence." Club memberships are also furnished. Indices provide access through family names that differ from the title, subsidiary titles (those different from the one by which a peer is known), name changes, and hyphenated names. Uniquely British in its unabashed emphasis on class.

232. Kidd, Charles, and Montague-Smith, Patrick. *Debrett's Book of Royal Children*. New York: William Morrow, 1982.

A history of British royal children, from Queen Victoria's brood through Prince William, first son of the current Prince and Princess of Wales.

233. Brough, James. *The Ford Dynasty: An American Story*. Garden City, NY: Doubleday, 1977.

A history of the Henry Ford family in the twentieth century.

234. Vidal, Gore, et al. *Great American Families.* New York: W. W. Norton, 1977.

Histories of six famous American families: the Adamses, Vanderbilts, Fords, Guggenheims, Roosevelts, and Rockefellers. The chapters trace each family's progress from its first rise to preeminence to its most recent noteworthy members. The book is heavily illustrated with portraits, photographs of locations, and painting reproductions. Includes an index but no bibliography.

235. Murray, Jane. *The Kings and Queens of England: A Tourist Guide.* New York: Charles Scribner's Sons, 1974.

Beginning with the present Queen Elizabeth II, Murray provides brief essays on each ruler of England back to Edward the Confessor, the first king to be buried in Westminster Abbey and the last of the old English line. Each entry is in narrative form and, though factual, is written in a lighthearted style.

236. Egan, Edward W.; Hintz, Constance B.; and Wise, L. F. *Kings, Rulers and Statesmen.* Rev. ed. New York: Sterling Publishing, 1976.

Arranged by nations, this book provides chronological lists of their rulers from each country's beginnings to the present. The administration, its dates, and any known events of importance that took place during that administration are listed.

237. Fraser, Antonia. *The Lives of the Kings and Queens of England.* New York: Knopf, 1975.

Divided into 10 sections, this work covers the monarchs of England from William I, 1066-87, through the modern House of Windsor. Each chapter covers a family or house, and genealogies accompany them. The coats of arms of each family are pictured in full color with each chapter, and an index provides access to individual names.

238. deCastries, Duc. *The Lives of the Kings and Queens of France.* Translated by Anne Dobell. New York: Alfred A. Knopf, 1979.

Divided into 7 parts, beginning with the Merovingians in the fifth century and concluding with the Orleans in 1848, this book traces the careers of those who occupied the French throne. Beautiful illustrations accompany the text, including painting and tapestry reproductions and sculptures. A glossary assists readers with French political terms, and there is an index.

239. Riddell, Edwin, and Laurence Urdang Associates. *Lives of the Stuart Age 1603-1714.* New York: Barnes and Noble, 1976.

Short biographical essays on prominent individuals in England during the Stuarts' reign.

240. Hoffman, Ann. *Lives of the Tudor Age 1485-1603.* New York: Barnes and Noble, 1977.

Contains 308 short sketches on prominent individuals of the Tudor reign in England. Some portraits are included, and a short list of sources follows each entry. There is an index and a classified index by profession.

241. Cleugh, James. *The Medici: A Tale of Fifteen Generations.* Garden City, NY: Doubleday, 1975.

> Provides background history of Florence, then focuses on the Medici family, covering the dynasty over almost 5 centuries. Chapters are divided by generations. Not a traditional biographical reference work, Cleugh's book is a scholarly monograph that would be useful to students of Florentine history, as well as Italian politics.

242. Tapsell, R. F. *Monarchs, Rulers, Dynasties and Kingdoms of the World.* New York: Facts on File, 1983.

> Although individual biographies do not appear on these pages, the alphabetical guide to dynasties and states provides broad biographical information on ruling families and dynasties. The Dynastic Lists section includes 254 nations/states/dynasties and the names of their rulers in chronological order.

243. Canning, John. *100 Great Kings, Queens, and Rulers of the World.* New York: Taplinger Publishing, 1967.

> A chronological guide to the most notable world leaders, beginning with Cheops and ending with John F. Kennedy. Sketches are the length of short chapters and are written in a casual, conversational style. There is an index.

244. Kaufman, Rosalie. *Queens of England.* 3 volumes. Chicago: The Warner Co., 1895.

> Chronological biographies of the Queens of England through Queen Victoria. Illustrated with engravings, the book is aimed at a juvenile Victorian audience. [Juvenile]

245. Lofts, Norah. *Queens of England.* Garden City, NY: Doubleday, 1977.

> Norah Lofts is well-known for her many books on tragic royal figures, particularly queens. This liberally illustrated volume includes English queens from Boadicea to Elizabeth II. Each entry indicates whether the queen was a ruler in her own right or the consort of a king. Birth, marriage, and death dates are listed, followed by a very readable biographical essay on the queen's life and times.

246. Moscow, Alvin. *The Rockefeller Inheritance.* Garden City, NY: Doubleday, 1977.

> A biography of the 5 Rockefeller brothers: John D. the Third, Nelson A., Laurance S., Winthrop, and David. The book is an exploration of how the most affluent people live and use their wealth as well as a biographical treatment of the Rockefellers' careers.

247. Morton, Frederic. *The Rothschilds: A Family Portrait.* New York: Atheneum, 1962.

> Traces the rise of the House of Rothschild from the 1760s to the 1960s, focusing on individual members of the family who influenced the spread and development of the dynasty. A fold-out genealogy of male descendants follows the text.

VII. Religion

248. Elder, Benedict, et al. *American Catholic Who's Who.* Washington, DC: National Catholic News Service. Irregular.

Contains over 5,000 sketches on American Roman Catholics, including the United States and its territories, as well as American-born Catholics living abroad. Church officials and other professionals are included, and women are well-represented in the entries. A list of the members of the National Conference of Catholic Bishops appears near the back, as does a geographical index of names. A short necrology concludes the work.

249. Attwater, Donald. *The Avenet Dictionary of Saints.* New York: Avenet Books, 1981.

Formerly titled *The Penguin Dictionary of Saints*, this is an alphabetical listing of saints, their histories, and feast days. The introduction provides a history of sainthood and explains canonization. There are a general bibliography and a glossary included, as well as a calendar of feast days.

250. Thurston, Herbert, and Attwater, Donald. *Butler's Lives of the Saints.* 4 volumes. 2d ed. rev. New York: P.J. Kennedy and Sons, 1962.

A revision of Alban Butler's original work, published in London between 1756 and 1759, this 4-volume set contains over 2,500 entries and is arranged chronologically by saints' days as they fall on the calendar. Essays include approximate vital dates, the saint's holy deeds, and references to other information on that saint. Volume 4 includes an alphabetical name index.

251. Delaney, John J. *Dictionary of American Catholic Biography.* Garden City, NY: Doubleday, 1984.

Biographies of deceased American Catholics who made a significant contribution to the church and/or nation. Entries range from bishops to comedienne Gracie Allen.

252. Bowden, Henry Warner. *Dictionary of American Religious Biography.* Westport, CT: Greenwood Press, 1977.

Sketches on 425 religious leaders of the United States. Entries include factual data as well as a critical discussion of the individual's influence on political, religious, and educational life in America. A bibliography of works by and about the person conclude each sketch. Appendix I lists entries by their denominational affiliation; appendix II lists them by place of birth. There is an index to names and concepts as well.

253. Davidson, Gustav. *A Dictionary of Angels including the Fallen Angels.* New York: Free Press, 1967.

Alphabetical listing of angels, their activity, and references indicating where additional information can be found on them. Many are very brief entries. Appendices give various angel groupings: celestial hierarchy, throne angels, and governing angels, to name a few examples. There's also a section on sigils, charts, pacts, and a bibliography of additional sources.

254. Delaney, John J., and Tobin, James Edward. *Dictionary of Catholic Biography.* Garden City, NY: Doubleday, 1961.

The foreword aptly describes this as "a single reference volume of biographical information on outstanding Catholics from the time of the apostles to the present day." Entries are short, containing brief factual data and references to the individual's contributions to Catholicism. Some entries cite additional resources. A short section on the saints as patrons and symbols in art follows the biographies and precedes a chronological chart of popes and rulers.

255. Delaney, John J. *Dictionary of Saints.* Garden City, NY: Doubleday, 1980.

The *Dictionary of Saints* provides legendary, mythological, and factual information about over 5,000 saints. All saints on the Roman Calendar are included, as well as those dropped from it because of insufficient information. Also covered are those who are not saints but are near canonization; these are indicated by titles such as "Blessed" or "Venerable."

An introductory discussion on the role of saints in history and religion opens the work and is "must" reading for users, as it explains how sainthood is achieved. The entries follow, in alphabetical order, with biographical information, including the year of the saint's death, his/her deeds leading to canonization, and myths and miracles attributed to him/her.

256. *Encyclopedia of Southern Baptists.* 4 volumes, including 2 supplement volumes. Nashville, TN: Boardman, 1958; supplements 1971, 1982.

An encyclopedia of biographies, terminology, philosophical concepts, and places of interest to American members of the Southern Baptist convention. The signed biographical sketches are interfiled alphabetically with the other articles. Only deceased "personalities" are included. There is a separate volume serving as a cumulative index to the 4-volume set.

257. Grant, Michael, and Hazel, John. *Gods and Mortals in Classical Mythology.* Springfield, MA: G. & C. Merriam Co., 1973.

An alphabetical guide to the numerous humans and deities who provide the basis for the Greek and Roman myths. Illustrations from contemporary and later art works pepper the text, and there are cross-references from Roman names to their Greek counterparts.

258. *Lives of the Saints.* See *Butler's Lives of the Saints* (250).

259. *Penguin Dictionary of Saints.* See *Avenet Dictionary of Saints* (249).

260. Hatfield, Edwin F. *The Poets of the Church.* Anson D. F. Randolph, 1884. Reprint. Detroit, MI: Gale Research, 1978.
The "hymn-writers" listed in this reprint are long dead and primarily British. There are 193 alphabetically arranged entries, written in a narrative style. The entries discuss the writer's principle works and give basic information about the life and work of the writer. Nearly every entry includes an example of the writer's work. Includes an index of hymns.

261. John, Eric. *The Popes: A Concise Biographical History.* New York: Hawthorn Books, 1964.
A chronological history of the papacy from Peter to Pope Paul VI. There are illustrations for each entry. Entries range in length from several pages to a short paragraph, depending on the pope's tenure and his impact on Church politics and doctrine.

262. Newland, Mary Reed. *The Saint Book: For Parents, Teachers, Homilists, Storytellers, and Children.* New York: Seabury Press, 1979.
Brief sketches of more than 55 saints, arranged by the dates of their feast days, focusing on personal details and factual incidents of their personal lives.

263. Habig, M.A. *Saints of the Americas.* Huntington, IN: Our Sunday Visitor, 1974.
Forty-five saints and *beati* from the Western Hemisphere are profiled.

264. McGinley, Phyllis. *Saint-Watching.* New York: Viking Press, 1982.
Essays on the character of selected saints. The index provides access to individual names as they are mentioned in the text. A list of saints, their dates, and feast days provides more factual information. *Saint-Watching* is intended more as entertaining reading than as reference literature.

265. Barker, William P. *Who's Who in Church History.* Grand Rapids, MI: Baker House, 1977.
More than 1,500 individuals from all walks of life who left a mark on church history are included. Each sketch indicates the person's achievements within the church.

266. Brush, John W. *Who's Who in Church History.* Boston: Whittemore Associates, Inc., 1962.
This slim volume includes a glossary of religious terms and short, illustrated biographical paragraphs on over 200 influential Christian leaders.

267. Beebe, Tom. *Who's Who in New Thought: Biographical Dictionary of New Thought.* Lakemont, GA: CSA Press, 1977.
A biographical treatment of the leaders of the New Thought movement founded by Phineas P. Quimby in the 1850s, this source also contains directory information for New Thought and affiliated churches.

268. *Who's Who in Religion.* Chicago: Marquis Who's Who, 1975–76.
Included in this volume of over 16,000 biographies are church officials, clergy, religious educators, and lay leaders from most denominations represented in North America.

269. Barr, George. *Who's Who in the Bible*. Middle Village, NY: Jonathan David, 1975.

Eighteen hundred personal names from the Bible are identified, with at least one Biblical citation provided.

270. Brownrigg, Ronald. *Who's Who in the New Testament*. London: Weidenfeld and Nicholson, 1971.

Introductory essays are followed by biographical sketches, some exceedingly brief, of personages in the New Testament. Translations of many names are given, and citations leading to references in the New Testament are provided.

271. Comay, Joan. *Who's Who in the Old Testament Together with the Apocrypha*. London: Weidenfeld and Nicolson, 1971.

An introduction and chronology, tying events to major Biblical characters, precede the biographical sketches. Some entries are very brief, others longer, but each cites location of the personality in the Old Testament. The meaning for many names is also indicated. The Old Testament entries are followed by an introduction to the Apocrypha, followed by the sketches of people in the Apocrypha with references showing where they can be found in the Apocrypha and including translations of many names.

272. Moyer, Elgin. *Wycliffe Biographical Dictionary of the Church*. Chicago: Moody Press, 1982.

A history of the Christian Church in biographical form. A chronological index and outline of church history provide a framework for the sketches, which constitute the body of the work.

VIII. Occupational Sources

273. Miles, Wyndham D. *American Chemists and Chemical Engineers.* Washington, DC: American Chemical Society, 1976.

Published during the American Chemical Society's centennial year, this volume contains biographies of approximately 500 scientists whose work in chemistry was remarkable or outstanding in some way. The signed sketches include additional bibliographical references and emphasize the chemists' contributions to science. No living people are profiled.

274. Roysdon, Christine, and Khatri, Linda A. *American Engineers of the Nineteenth Century: A Biographical Index.* New York: Garland, 1978.

This index is a valuable guide to some of the practitioners of applied science in the last century. The individual's field of interest is indicated in addition to the life dates. Citations to additional biographical information—obituaries and biographies—are included. The last 2 decades of the nineteenth century are covered best.

275. *American Men and Women of Science.* New York: R. R. Bowker.

The 15th edition of *American Men and Women of Science: Physical and Biological Sciences* was published in 7 volumes in 1982. The biographical data are in "Who's Who" style—very abbreviated and precise. The 1982 volumes contain 130,000 individuals from the U.S. and Canada. *American Men and Women of Science* is now available online.

By popular request, a separate volume of *American Men and Women of Science* was published (most recently in 1978) in which 24,000 individuals in certain social and behavioral disciplines were pulled out from the so-called "hard sciences." *American Men and Women of Science: Social and Behavorial Sciences* includes 12 areas: administration and management; area studies; business; communications and information science; community and urban studies; economics; environmental studies; futuristics; international studies; political science; psychology; and sociology. Some "social" sciences were included in the other volumes of the series, including anthropology, geography, statistics, psychiatry, public health, and computer sciences.

276. Asimov, Isaac. *Asimov's Biographical Encyclopedia of Science and Technology: The Lives and Achievements of 1510 Great Scientists from Ancient Times to the Present Chronologically Arranged.* 2d ed. rev. Garden City, NY: Doubleday, 1982.

Coverage in this book begins with Imhotep, an Egyptian scholar who flourished from 2980–2950 B.C. and ends with Stephen William Hawking, an English physicist born in 1942. This biographical work is intended to serve as a history of science as much as a guide to the lives of the people involved in its study. Sketches emphasize each person's educational training, major contributions to science, and any awards received for research. Arranged chronologically, the book has an alphabetical listing of the biographees to aid in access. Cross-references to other sketches enhance the book's usefulness. An index provides access to names, places, and ideas cited in the work.

277. Ingham, John N. *Biographical Dictionary of American Business Leaders.* 4 volumes. Westport, CT: Greenwood Press, 1983.
Some still-living leaders are included here, but the emphasis is on significant leaders of the business community from America's history; 1,100 figures are covered. Entries give biographical and bibliographical information. Appendices provide access to the entries by place of birth or business, religion, birth year, sex, company and industry, and ethnic background.

278. Fink, Gary M. *Biographical Dictionary of American Labor Leaders.* Westport, CT: Greenwood Press, 1974.
The bulk of this work is made up of approximately 500 career biographies of men and women who have had a significant role in the American labor movement. Each biography includes major accomplishments, significant dates, family background, trade union affiliations, and offices held (both public and private). In addition, each biography includes bibliographical references to primary and secondary sources which provide further information.
Special appendices arrange the biographees by the following topics: union affiliations, religious preference, place of birth, formal education, political preference, and major appointive and elective public offices. There is also a comprehensive subject index.

279. Elliot, Clark A. *Biographical Dictionary of American Science: The Seventeenth Through the Nineteenth Centuries.* Westport, CT: Greenwood Press, 1979.
This work includes narrative biographies of scientists born between 1606 and 1867. Full biographical information is provided for the almost 600 scientists profiled. Appendices provide listings by years of birth, place of birth, education, and fields of science.

280. Pleasants, Helene. *Biographical Dictionary of Parapsychology with Directory and Glossary.* New York: Garrett Publications, 1964.
A dictionary/directory of Americans concerned with psychic research. Entries include vital data and educational background, as well as a statement of research interests and an address.

281. Zusne, Leonard. *Biographical Dictionary of Psychology.* Westport, CT: Greenwood, 1984.
This is a revision of *Names in the History of Psychology*, also by Zusne. Over 600 entries are included with key biographical data provided as well as the contribution made by the individual, or the theory to which s/he subscribed, and any major publications or other contributions made during his/her career.

282. Williams, Trevor. *A Biographical Dictionary of Scientists.* 3d ed. New York: John Wiley, 1982.

Deceased scientists of note are discussed in short narrative versions of their lives and contributions. Citations are provided so readers can pursue further information on the individuals.

283. Daintith, John; Mitchell, Sarah; and Toothill, Elizabeth. *A Biographical Encyclopedia of Scientists.* 2 volumes. New York: Facts on File, 1981.

Concentrating on the "traditional" pure sciences—physics, chemistry, biology, astronomy and the earth sciences," and including mathematics, engineering, and technology, this work endeavors to profile scientists from the beginning of scientific inquiry to the present. The brief entries include educational background, significant contributions to science, and awards won. More than 2,000 individuals are included. In addition to name and subject indices, there is a chronology and a reading list.

284. Weisberger, Bernard A. *Captains of Industry.* New York: American Heritage, 1966.

The "Captains of Industry" profiled here are 10 Americans who spurred the Industrial Revolution in the United States: Cornelius Vanderbilt, Cyrus McCormick, Philip Armour, James B. Duke, James J. Hill, Meyer Guggenheim, John D. Rockefeller, J. P. Morgan, Andrew Carnegie, and Henry Ford. Written for late elementary to early secondary school-aged children, the profiles in this book are arranged into 7 chapters, each addressing a different aspect of industrialization. [Juvenile]

285. Gillispie, Charles Coulston. *Dictionary of Scientific Biography.* 16 volumes. New York: Charles Scribner's Sons, 1970.

This work attempts to deal with the history of science through providing biographical information on scientists. It covers all periods from classical antiquity to the present. Living persons are not included. In selecting names for inclusion, the editors attempted to "include articles on those figures whose contributions to science were sufficiently distinctive to make an identifiable difference to the profession or community of knowledge." Articles are signed, and most include bibliographies of works by and about the biographee. Volume 16 includes the index as well as lists of societies, periodicals indexed, and a list of scientists arranged by field.

286. Hebert, Robert F., and Link, Albert N. *The Entrepreneurs: Mainstream Views and Radical Critiques.* New York: Praeger, 1982.

The authors provide biographical information on a dozen or so entrepreneurs who have left their mark on the history of economics and finance. Although not strictly biographies, the sketches provide valuable secondary biographical information. There's a bibliography and a name index.

287. Bolton, Sarah K. *Famous Men of Science.* Revised by Barbara Lovett Cline. New York: Thomas Y. Crowell, 1960.

Twenty-three famous scientists, including Marie Curie, are profiled in brief narratives.

288. Freeman, T. W., et al. *Geographers: Biobibliographical Studies.*
London: Mansell, 1977–.
These narrative biographies of major geographers are followed by bibliographies and other sources and a life chronology. The title of this series varies and sometimes includes the phrase "On behalf of the International Geographical Union Commission on the History of Geographical Thought."

289. Turner, Roland; Goulden, Stephen L.; and Sheridan, Barbara.
Great Engineers and Pioneers in Technology: From Antiquity through the Industrial Revolution. New York: St. Martin's Press, 1981.
Entries are organized into 5 sections, arranged by time period, and emphasize the achievements of the biographees. Each section is introduced by an essay describing the period and the events of the time. There is a glossary of technical terms and a bibliography. People born through 1799 are included.

290. Ireland, Norma Olin. *Index to Scientists of the World from Ancient to Modern Times: Biographies and Portraits.* Boston: F. W. Faxon, 1962.
Indexes over 300 biographical dictionaries containing sketches on living and deceased scientists.

291. Sills, David L. *International Encyclopedia of the Social Sciences—Biographical Supplement.* New York: The Free Press, 1979.
Presents biographies of 215 distinguished social scientists. Coverage is international, and both living and deceased scholars are included. In addition to personal information, the sketches include an analysis of the biographee's contributions to the social sciences and a lengthy bibliography of works by and about the individual.

292. *McGraw-Hill Modern Scientists and Engineers.* 2d ed. 3 volumes.
New York: McGraw-Hill, 1980.
Covering the twentieth century through 1978, this work profiles scientists and engineers. Both living and dead people are listed in the entries. Most are Americans; whether that reflects a publisher's bias or a technological one is up to the reader. A scope note indicates that, whenever possible, subjects were asked to submit writings about their work for the profiles. Cross-references to the *McGraw-Hill Encyclopedia of Science and Technology* make the book quite useful to those doing introductory research.

293. *Martindale-Hubbell Law Directory.* 115th ed. 7 volumes.
Summit, NJ: Martindale-Hubbell, Inc., 1984. Frequency varies.
Arranged geographically, then alphabetically, this directory provides information about law firms and attorneys throughout the U.S. Biographical information is brief, but potentially useful, and includes educational background, date of admission to the bar, and a list of the firm's representative clients.

294. Mai, Ludwig H. *Men and Ideas in Economics: A Dictionary of World Economists Past and Present.* Totowa, NJ: Rowman and Littlefield, 1977.
Provides biographical sketches of economic theorists from all Western cultures, including such diverse people as popes, statesmen, physicians,

jurists, and writers. Historical coverage is extensive, including representatives from the fourth century to the present. A short introduction, entitled "The Growth of Economic Thought," precedes 248 pages of paragraph-long sketches. Each profile includes vital dates, the subject's primary profession, and a brief description of that person's contribution to economic theory. The appendices provide, respectively, an essay on current economists, an outline of periods and schools of economic theory, and a bibliography.

295. Riedman, Sarah R. *Men and Women Behind the Atom.* London: Abelard-Schuman, 1958.
Readable narratives covering contributions and personal lives of the men and women behind atomic research are grouped into 14 chapters. Individuals included range from the Curies to Oppenheimer.

296. Bell, E. T. *Men of Mathematics.* New York: Simon and Schuster, 1965.
This work is written in a style for general readers, not scholars, and is not intended to be a history of mathematics. The period covered is fifth-century B.C. to the early nineteenth century: Babylonian, Greek, Newtonian, and the Golden Age of Mathematics (1800 to the present). Entire chapters are devoted to some of the greats of mathematics such as Newton. Profiles cover contributions to the field as well as their personal trials and tribulations.

297. Thomas, Shirley. *Men of Space: Profiles of the Leaders in Space Research, Development, and Exploration.* 8 volumes. Philadelphia, PA: Chilton, 1960–68.
Includes factual and lengthy biographies of prominent figures in space research.

298. De Kruif, Paul Henry. *The Microbe Hunters.* New York: Harcourt, Brace, & Co., 1954.
Chapter-length biographies of 14 scientists and physicians who helped eradicate disease in humans by tracking down elusive microorganisms that were the carriers of illness.

299. Zusne, Leonard. *Names in the History of Psychology: A Biographical Sourcebook.* New York: Halstead, 1975.
Arranged chronologically by birth date, this work profiles 526 deceased contributors to psychology and its development through history. Other biographical sources of additional information are included.

300. Ross, Keyo. *National Directory of Certified Public Accountants and Accounting Firms.* Princeton, NJ: Peter Norback Publishing, 1981–.
Although the directory portion of this work is patterned after the law firm information in the *Martindale-Hubbell Law Directory*, there is a 287-page-long biographical section, which includes each accountant's professional affiliation, degrees, and memberships.

301. Feldman, Anthony, and Ford, Peter. *Scientists and Inventors.* New York: Facts on File, 1979.
The time period covered ranges from B.C. to the time of publication and includes more than 150 scientists and inventors. Arrangement is

chronological with biographical information and contributions made by
the individuals included in the sketches. Access is facilitated through an
alphabetical list of people included as well as an index.

302. *Standard and Poor's Register of Corporations, Directors and
Executives.* New York: Standard and Poor's. Annual.
A 3-volume guide to the chief executives and other high-ranking officers
and headquarter locations of major American corporations. Volume 1
provides listings by corporation name; volume 2 is an alphabetical listing
of the directors and executives of those businesses. Biographical information is minimal: Each person's principle business affiliation, birth date,
college and graduate degrees and dates, and his/her address are listed, as
well as any other business appointments and professional memberships.
Volume 3 lists business leaders who died during the previous year and
those individuals who are new to the directory.

303. *Who Was Who in American History—Science and Technology.*
Chicago: Marquis Who's Who, 1976.
Includes 10,000 deceased scientists and other technologists prominent in
the early 1970s.

304. *Who's Who in Atoms 1960.* London: Vallancey Press, 1960.
Contains 125,000 concise biographical entries. Though now very out-
dated, this work does indicate the state of the field in 1960.

305. Wasserman, Paul, and McLear, Janice. *Who's Who in
Consulting: A Reference Guide to Professional Personnel Engaged in
Consultation for Business, Industry and Government.* 2d ed. Detroit,
MI: Gale Research, 1973.
A biographical guide to business consultants, this book also provides
access to names by region and area of expertise.

306. Gregory, Jean. *Who's Who in Engineering.* 3d ed. New York:
Engineers Joint Council, 1977.
U.S. engineers are listed in concise biographical entries. Included also are
listings of societies and awards, groupings of individuals by specializa-
tion, and a geographic index.

307. *Who's Who in Finance and Industry.* 23d ed. Chicago: Marquis
Who's Who, 1983–84. Biannual.
Lists approximately 22,600 entries, including "qualified men and women
in all lines of useful and reputable financial endeavor." Coverage encom-
passes all of North America; a "Professional Index" provides name
access under 250 professional subject headings.

308. Wolff, Donald E. *Who's Who in Insurance.* Englewood, NJ:
Underwriter Printing and Publishing Co. Annual.
Gives short biographical entries on individuals prominent in the insur-
ance business.

309. *Who's Who in Labor.* New York: Arno Press, 1976.
Biographies of individuals currently active in the labor movement at the
time of publication. All unions and organizations in America are represented; officeholders of those groups comprise the majority of the entries.
Labor analysts, scholars, and journalists are also included. A reference

section at the end of the book includes a directory of unions and employee associations, government labor offices, and a bibliography of labor periodicals.

310. Tunucci, Barbara A. *Who's Who in Technology Today.* 5 volumes. Lake Bluff, IL: J. Dick Publisher, 1984.
A biographical directory of technological researchers and innovators. The 5 volumes are divided by area of specialty: (1) Electronics and Computer Science; (2) Physics and Optics; (3) Chemistry and Biotechnology; (4) Mechanical, Civil, Energy and Earth Science; and (5) Index. The index volume includes an index of principle expertise and a name index.

311. *Who's Who in World Agriculture.* 2 volumes. Harlow, England: Francis Hodgson, 1979.
This work is based on the *Agricultural Research Index*, which is a directory of agricultural research institutes. In addition to people named in the *Index*, the editors have selected additional names of heads of university departments, officers of national and international associations, and agricultural journal editors. Over 140 countries are represented.

312. Osen, Lynn M. *Women in Mathematics.* Cambridge, MA: MIT Press, 1974.
Eight women whose theories contributed to the study of mathematics are profiled here, beginning with Hypatia, a Greek woman who flourished in the fourth century, and concluding with Emmy (Amalie) Noether, who died in 1935. The book's first chapter offers a history of the female role in mathematical studies. Two other chapters which follow the biographical sections provide some perspective on the decline of female involvement in mathematical theory. Illustrations accompany most entries, and a bibliography and index conclude the volume.

IX. Education-Related Sources

313. *Academic Who's Who: University Teachers in the British Isles in the Arts, Education and Social Sciences.* 2d ed. London: Adams & Charles Black, 1975.

> This work covers scholars in universities in the British Isles who hold the rank of senior lecturer or above or who have taught for 5 years as a lecturer or assistant lecturer. The 7,000 entries are brief listings of career information.

314. Ohles, John F. *Biographical Dictionary of American Educators.* 3 volumes. Westport, CT: Greenwood Press, 1978.

> This biographical dictionary covers educators who have been involved significantly in American education from the colonial period to the Bicentennial. There are entries for 1,665 educators. The sketches are narrative discussions of the careers of these educators. Appendices provide listings of the educators by place of birth, specialization, main state of employment, and dates important in American education.

315. Ash, Lee. *Biographical Directory of Librarians in the United States and Canada.* 5th ed. Chicago: American Library Association, 1970.

> Brief biographical data are provided on librarians active at the time of publication.

316. Cummings, Cynthia S. *A Biographical-Bibliographical Directory of Women Librarians.* Madison, WI: University of Wisconsin-Madison, Library School Women's Group, 1976.

> A compilation intended as a "reference tool of historical perspective, aimed at gathering together not only the personal data of significant leaders of the past, but also the bibliographical citations...." Though now out of date, this does serve as a resource of data on several women active in the library profession in the past. Entries indicate where additional data can be found.

317. Wynar, Bohdan S. *Dictionary of American Library Biography.* Littleton, CO: Libraries Unlimited, Inc., 1978.

> Librarians who achieved "professional distinction," held positions of national importance, or made other contributions that profoundly affected librarianship are included in this biographical dictionary. These 300 sketches are posthumous biographies. Highlights of each librarian's professional career comprise the main body of each entry.

318. Jacques Cattell Press. *Directory of American Scholars.* 7th ed. 4 volumes. New York: R. R. Bowker, 1978.
Begun in 1942 as a humanities and social sciences companion to *American Men of Science* (now *American Men and Women of Science*), the seventh edition of the work includes nearly 40,000 entries. Most are of college and university faculty members, although some independent scholars are included. The 4 volumes of the *Directory* cover broad disciplines: volume 1, History; volume 2, English, Speech, and Drama; volume 3, Foreign Languages, Linguistics and Philology; volume 4, Philosophy, Religion, and Law. A geographic index for each volume provides access by state and city.

319. Jacques Cattell Press. *Leaders in Education.* 5th ed. New York: R. R. Bowker, 1974.
Almost 17,000 biographies of educators are included with selections based on these criteria: achievement of a level equivalent to that associated with the doctoral degree plus activities; high-quality research activity; and position of substantial responsibility.

320. *National Faculty Directory 1984: An Alphabetical List, with Addresses, of about 597,000 Members of Teaching Faculties at Junior Colleges, Colleges, and Universities in the United States and at Selected Canadian Institutions.* 14th ed. 3 volumes. Detroit, MI: Gale Research, 1983.
The subtitle of this directory explains its contents. No biographical information is included, but this annual publication can be quite useful for people trying to locate colleagues in higher education.

321. Landau, Thomas. *Who's Who in Librarianship.* London: Bowes and Bowes, 1954–.
Biographies of British librarians. Later editions (1972–) are entitled *Who's Who in Librarianship and Information Science.*

322. Lee, Joel M. *Who's Who in Library and Information Services.* Chicago: American Library Association, 1982.
A directory of librarians who are active professionally, both in publication activity and in the library professional associations.

323. Ash, Lee. *Who's Who in Library Service.* 4th ed. Hamden, CT: Shoe String Press, 1966.
Published by the Advisory Committee of National Library Associations, this is a precursor to the modern *Who's Who in Library and Information Services.*

X. Sports

324. Soderberg, Paul, and Washington, Helen. *The Big Book of Halls of Fame in the United States and Canada: Sports*. New York: R. R. Bowker, 1977.
> All inductees of any sports hall of fame in North America that has strict membership election standards are included. Thirty sports activities are covered, and there is a Special Fields section for other types of sports Halls of Fame. Sports covered are: angling, archery, automobile racing, baseball, basketball, bicycling, billiards, bird racing and breeding, bowling, boxing, dogs and dog racing, football, golf, hockey, horse racing and breeding, horseshoe pitching, hunting, ice skating, lacrosse, martial arts, roller skating, shuffleboard, skiing, soccer, softball, tennis, track and field, trapshooting, water sports, and wrestling. Includes Halls of Fame where animals as well as people are inducted.

325. Smith, Robert. *Pioneers of Baseball*. Boston: Little, Brown, 1978.
> This book traces the development of this most American game from its roots in nineteenth- century New York City to the 1950s. Sixteen players are discussed, ranging from Alexander Cartwright, who is credited with inventing the game (not Abner Doubleday), to Ted Williams. [Juvenile]

326. Mallon, Bill; Buchanan, Ian; and Tishman, Jeffrey. *Quest for Gold: The Encyclopedia of American Olympians*. New York: Scribner's, 1984.
> Mostly brief sketches covering the medal winners from the 1896 games to the 1980 Moscow games, which the U.S. boycotted. Appendices list Olympic records and a sport-by-sport index.

327. Clark, Patrick. *Sports Firsts*. New York: Facts on File, 1981.
> Sports firsts and record performances are included in 18 chapters, with major sports having entire chapters of their own.

328. Hickok, Ralph. *Who Was Who in American Sports*. New York: Hawthorn Books, 1971.
> A history of American sports through some of its more memorable characters. Only deceased individuals are included, and all sports are represented.

329. Mendell, Ronald L. *Who's Who in Basketball*. New Rochelle, NY: Arlington House, 1973.
> Includes more than 900 basketball participants from the late nineteenth century to the time of publication. Award winners, players, coaches, officials, and others with some connection to the development of bas-

ketball as a major sport are included. The entries are brief, with such data as height being included.

330. Burrill, Bob. *Who's Who in Boxing.* New Rochelle, NY: Arlington House, 1974.

Includes profiles of promoters and managers as well as boxers from the sport's inception to the early 1970s. Listed are major fights, career records, and their size.

331. Mendell, Ronald, and Phares, Timothy B. *Who's Who in Football.* New Rochelle, NY: Arlington House, 1974.

Gives short, factual data on the greats of American collegiate and professional football, from the late 1800s to the early 1970s. Living and deceased players, coaches, owners, and managers are included.

332. Alliss, Peter. *The Who's Who of Golf.* Englewood Cliffs, NJ: Prentice-Hall, 1983.

An international guide to the greats of golfing, both past and present. The book is broken into 8 geographical divisions, and sketches are arranged alphabetically within those groupings. Photographs accompany most sketches, and each entry includes a brief résumé of the person's winning record and prize earnings.

XI. Medicine

333. American Medical Association. *American Medical Directory: Directory of Physicians in the United States, Canal Zone, Puerto Rico, Virgin Islands, Certain Pacific Islands and U.S. Physicians Temporarily Located in Foreign Countries.* Compiled for the Association by Jacques Cattell Press and R. R. Bowker Company. 4 volumes. 28th ed. Chicago: American Medical Association, 1982.

A directory of physicians in the geographic areas indicated in the subtitle. Volume 1 lists each physician alphabetically by name and indicates what city s/he lives in. Volumes 2 through 4 list geographic locations with physicians' names, addresses, and codes indicating their medical school, specialty, and type of practice.

334. Talbott, John Harold. *A Biographical History of Medicine: Excerpts and Essays on the Men and Their Work.* New York: Grune & Stratton, 1970.

Originally published in the *Journal of the American Medical Association*, these biographies include some twentieth-century personages but primarily cover people prior to this century. Individuals included are discussed with emphasis on their writings and their accomplishments. A bibliography at the end of each entry lists their writings or writings about them. There is a name and a subject index to facilitate access.

335. Kaufman, Martin; Galishoff, Stuart; and Savitt, Todd L. *Dictionary of American Medical Biography.* 2 volumes. Westport, CT: Greenwood, 1984.

One should not assume from the title that this work covers only physicians. The important doctors who were leaders in their field are listed but also included are major figures in related medical fields: nursing and public health, for example. Covering the seventeenth century through 1977, nontraditional medicine is also represented in the form of sects and healers. Basic biographical information is included in the entries; a bibliography covers publications for each entry where relevant.

336. *Directory of Medical Specialists.* 19th ed. 3 volumes. Chicago: Marquis Who's Who, 1979–80.

A geographical directory of physicians specializing in a particular area of medicine. Ranging from allergy to urology, the 3-volume set lists practitioners by state, then city, under their area of specialty. A short list of credentials follows each physician's name.

337. Gilbert, Judson Bennett, and Mestler, Gordon E. *Disease and Destiny: A Bibliography of Medical References to the Famous.* London: Dawson's of Pall Mall, 1962.

This book contains medical articles, listed alphabetically by name of subject, about the illnesses of famous people. For the people included, life dates and a brief phrase describing the person's occupation and nationality are provided.

338. Editorial Staff of Francis Hodgson Reference Publications. *International Medical Who's Who: A Biographical Guide for Medical Research.* 2 volumes. London: Francis Hodgson, 1980.

Included are more than 12,000 people from more than 120 countries. Information is in brief form, mainly indicating education and specialty areas.

339. De Kruif, Paul. *Men Against Death.* New York: Harcourt, Brace, 1932.

Presents biographies of 12 physicians who made major contributions toward conquering "incurable" diseases. Author De Kruif read each man's publications and studied his research before interviewing him for the book. There is an index of names and subjects at the book's end and portraits of the subjects are included.

XII. Writers

340. Burke, W. J., and Howe, Will D. Revised by Irving Weiss and Ann Weiss. *American Authors and Books: 1640 to the Present Day.* 3d rev. ed. New York: Crown Publishers, 1972.

Authors and works in American literature are briefly identified. The compilers state that every effort has been made to cover trends of recent years as well as scholarly works. Living and dead authors are covered. Entries are brief, listing name, dates, occupation, and most important works. There are entries on trends in which relevant works are cited, and entries about publishers, indicating each house's field of concentration.

341. Kunitz, Stanley J., and Haycraft, Howard. *American Authors 1600-1900.* New York: H. W. Wilson, 1938.

This volume covers the period 1607 to 1900 and contains biographical sketches of authors involved in making U.S. literary history. There are 1,300 entries with each one including the author's principal works, dates of publication, and a list of biographical and critical sources.

342. Elliot, Emory. *American Colonial Writers, 1606-1734.* Detroit, MI: Gale Research, 1984.

While we are familiar with many of the writers of this period, such as Cotton Mather, Roger Williams, Jonathan Edwards, and Benjamin Franklin, lesser-known authors of the colonial period are also included among the 95 writers covered by biographical/critical essays. A bibliography accompanies each entry. This is volume 24 of the Dictionary of Literary Biography series.

343. ———. *American Colonial Writers, 1735-1781.* Detroit, MI: Gale Research, 1984.

This is a continuation of the theme first undertaken by the editor in a volume covering the years 1606-1734. Sixty-two Americans are profiled in essays that cover the careers of the authors and critique their contributions to American literature. The events of the period during which the writers were productive can be seen through the essays, which include bibliographies of each author's works. This is volume 31 of the Dictionary of Literary Biography series.

344. Wilson, Clyde N. *American Historians, 1607-1865.* Detroit, MI: Gale Research, 1984.

This guide to American historiography covers 46 practitioners of historical research. A selected bibliography is included for each as well as the standard data; a list of books for further reading is also included in the volume. This is volume 30 of the Dictionary of Literary Biography series.

345. Trachtenberg, Stanley. *American Humorists, 1800–1950.* 2 volumes. Detroit, MI: Gale Research, 1982.

Seventy-two literary humorists are included in essays detailing their lives and contributions. The essays are accompanied by lists of each person's works, as well as bibliographies for additional reading. This is volume 11 of the Dictionary of Literary Biography series.

346. Traub, Hamilton. *The American Literary Yearbook: A Biographical Dictionary of Living North American Authors.* Henning, MN: H. Traub, 1919. Reprint. Detroit, MI: Gale Research, 1968.

Preceding the title page of this reprint is the following bibliographical note: "Though intended to be an annual publication, the 1919 volume of *The American Literary Yearbook* was the only one published."

Traub's aim in 1919 was to "set down a comprehensive record of present literary activity in North America." In his first and only volume of the *Yearbook*, he included a calendar of literary events, through which readers can note birth and death dates of authors as well as landmark publication dates. Also included are a listing of new books published in North America in 1918, arranged by Traub's own subject scheme, cross indexes from pseudonym to given name and back, and a statistical list of birthplaces and residences of contemporary authors. One section of the book consists of short biographical sketches of writers alive in 1918. In another section, Traub provides a list of literary institutions in North America, including the American Academy of Arts and Letters, club and association prizes, and research libraries in North America. Still another part is an author's manual, including everything an aspiring author needed to know about publishing, from type sizes and typefaces to which publishers specialize in particular subject areas.

347. Ashley, Perry J. *American Newspaper Journalists, 1873–1900.* Detroit, MI: Gale Research, 1983.

These essays on 42 journalists describe their journalism careers as well as biographical information. Some of their publications are included, and there is a list of works to read for additional information on this developmental period of American journalism. This is volume 23 of the Dictionary of Literary Biography series.

348. ———. *American Newspaper Journalists, 1901–1925.* Detroit, MI: Gale Research, 1984.

This title continues the coverage begun in the volume that covers the years 1873–1900. As the new century began, and prior to the Depression, journalism became very colorful and active. Forty-seven journalists are profiled with biographical and bibliographical information. An additional reading list is included. This is volume 25 of the Dictionary of Literary Biography series.

349. Martine, James J. *American Novelists, 1910–1945.* 3 volumes. Detroit, MI: Gale Research, 1981.

Included in this volume are 125 novelists from this tumultuous period in American history. Since this was a period of activity for many of our greatest novelists, the user will find entries for Dos Passos, Cather,

O'Hara, Fitzgerald, Hemingway, and many other well-known writers.
Entries include a bibliography of the author's work, an essay about
him/her, and a bibliography of other publications which could assist the
researcher. This is volume 9 of the Dictionary of Literary Biography
series.

350. Warfell, Harry R. *American Novelists of Today*. New York:
American Book Co., 1951. Reprint. Westport, CT: Greenwood Press,
1976.
A compilation of 575 sketches of American novelists living in 1951.
Arranged alphabetically, each sketch includes biographical information,
the author's works of fiction, and his/her statement of purpose or philosophy. A brief description of each novel concludes the sketch.

351. Helterman, Jeffrey, and Layman, Richard. *American Novelists
Since World War II*. Detroit, MI: Gale Research, 1978.
Eighty novelists are covered in critical essays with bibliographies of
relevant materials by and about the authors. This volume is
supplemented by Kibler's work (see following entry) of the same title.
This is volume 2 of the Dictionary of Literary Biography series.

352. Kibler, James E., Jr. *American Novelists Since World War II,
Second Series*. Detroit, MI: Gale Research, 1980.
Seventy novelists are profiled in essays, which are followed by a bibliog-
raphy of works by and about each of them. This work supplements the
earlier volume by Helterman and Layman. This is volume 6 of the
Dictionary of Literary Biography series.

353. Greiner, Donald J. *American Poets Since World War II*. 2
volumes. Detroit, MI: Gale Research, 1980.
Includes 125 poets, with critical essays of their works, lists of their
works, and sources for additional reading about each poet. This volume
also includes a cumulative list of entries for the first 5 volumes of the
Dictionary of Literary Biography series. This is volume 5 of the Dictionary of Literary Biography series.

354. Pizer, Donald, and Harbert, Earl N. *American Realists and
Naturalists*. Detroit, MI: Gale Research, 1982.
The period of realism and naturalism is usually placed between the end
of the Civil War and the beginning of World War I. This volume follows
the usual format of volumes in the Dictionary of Literary Biography
series with critical essays on 42 individuals and sources of additional
information for the researcher. This is volume 12 of the Dictionary of
Literary Biography series.

355. Myerson, Joel. *The American Renaissance in New England*.
Detroit, MI: Gale Research, 1978.
Ninety-eight authors are included in essays accompanied by bibliographical information for additional research. This, volume 1 of the Dictionary of Literary Biography series, marked the debut of this series.

356. Morsberger, Robert E.; Lesser, Stephen O.; and Clark, Randall.
American Screenwriters. Detroit, MI: Gale Research, 1984.
Lengthy essays discuss the careers of 65 screenwriters. Included are
people who wrote primarily for film; excluded are those better known for

other writing pursuits but who did some screenwriting. A bibliography provides additional sources for further reading. This is volume 26 of the Dictionary of Literary Biography series.

357. Unger, Leonard, and Litz, A. Walton. *American Writers: A Collection of Literary Biographies.* 8 volumes, some of which are supplements. New York: Scribner's, 1979.
Originally published as the *University of Minnesota Pamphlets on American Writers.* Included are essays on American writers living and dead during the period from Colonial America to 1972. Three-fourths of the writers are from the twentieth century. Each entry consists of a formal essay by a recognized writer, a selected bibliography, and a list of critical and biographical studies.

358. Levernier, James A., and Wilmes, Douglas R. *American Writers Before 1800: A Biographical and Critical Dictionary.* Westport, CT: Greenwood Press, 1983.
Just as in the *American Colonial Writers* volumes in the Dictionary of Literary Biography series from Gale, this work also includes minor writers as well as the familiar—Benjamin Franklin, Cotton Mather, Jonathan Edwards. Over 700 people are included in biographical and bibliographical entries that include some criticism and judgment of the author's influence.

359. Cech, John. *American Writers for Children, 1900–1960.* Detroit, MI: Gale Research, 1983.
This volume capitalizes on one of the periods of greatest productivity in the field of children's literature. Forty-three authors of the period are included with the usual biographical narrative, including commentary on the author's body of work, and followed by a selective bibliography. This is volume 22 of the Dictionary of Literary Biography series.

360. Rood, Karen Lane. *American Writers in Paris 1920–1939.* Detroit, MI: Gale Research, 1980.
Ninety-nine expatriate American writers who based their activity in Paris are discussed in critical essays. Each entry also includes the writer's major publications. This is volume 4 of the Dictionary of Literary Biography series.

361. Myerson, Joel. *Antebellum Writers in New York and the South.* Detroit, MI: Gale Research, 1979.
The period 1820–60 signaled change and approaching upheaval in American society. Two active literary fronts were New York and the South. Over 60 writers of this period are covered in essays accompanied by appropriate bibliographies. This is volume 3 of the Dictionary of Literary Biography series.

362. McNeil, Barbara, and Herbert, Miranda C. *Author Biographies Master Index: A Consolidated Guide to More than 658,000 Biographical Sketches Concerning Authors Living and Dead as They Appear in a Selection of the Principal Biographical Dictionaries Devoted to Authors, Poets, Journalists and Other Literary Figures.* 2 volumes. Detroit, MI: Gale Research, 1984.

An index to biographical dictionaries of authors and writers. Names are entered alphabetically, with life dates and abbreviations to indicate which biographical works include information on that writer.

363. *Publishers Weekly* Editors and Contributors. *The Author Speaks: Selected "PW" Interviews, 1967–1976.* New York: R. R. Bowker, 1977.
This collection of 154 interviews captures the best of a *Publishers Weekly* feature. The interviews are divided into 6 categories by the types of work the author writes: Novels and Short Stories; Mystery and Suspense; Biography (the authors talk about their subjects); Autobiography; Letters and Memoirs; Current Social Concerns and Commentary; and History and Political Commentary.
    The interviews are not biographies in the classic sense, but each piece contains valuable insights into the life and work of the writer.

364. *The Author's and Writer's Who's Who.* 6th ed. London: Burke's Peerage, Ltd., 1971; Darien, CT: Hafner Publishing, 1971.
More than 10,000 brief biographical sketches of living authors and writers in North America and the British Isles are included. A list of pseudonyms refers readers to writers' given names, under which the entries will be found.

365. Hoffman, Miriam, and Samuels, Eva. *Authors and Illustrators of Children's Books: Writings on their Lives and Works.* New York: R. R. Bowker, 1972.
The 50 essays contained in this book are both biographical and critical; bibliographical sources conclude each. The editors also insert a note at the end of each containing additional biographical data and their comments on the biographees' works. These essays or readings are reprinted from other sources and are often based on actual interviews with the individuals. The appendix lists the English language works of each author and author-illustrator.

366. Nykorvk, Barbara. *Authors in the News: A Compilation of News Stories and Feature Articles from American Newspapers and Magazines Covering Writers and Other Members of the Communications Media.* 2 volumes. Detroit, MI: Gale Research, 1976.
About 500 writers are covered in this 2-volume set. Primarily magazine writers, newspaper reporters, columnists, and television writers are included. The list of newspapers and magazines from which the entries were taken is at the front of each volume along with an index listing the people covered. The entries themselves are reprints of newspaper and magazine articles. These are not full biographical sketches but often provide vignettes on the lives of sometimes-obscure writers.

367. Ward, Martha E., and Marquardt, Dorothy A. *Authors of Books for Young People.* 2d ed. 1 volume plus supplement volume. Metuchen, NJ: Scarecrow, 1971–79.
Included are all recipients of the Newbery and Caldecott Awards through 1978. The biographical information is based on the "author file" compiled in the children's department of the Free Public Library in Quincy, IL.

368. Charters, Ann. *The Beats: Literary Bohemians in Postwar America*. Detroit, MI: Gale Research, 1983.
Over 60 writers of the period who might be characterized as "beats" are profiled in critical essays accompanied by lists of the works of the writers and sources of additional reading. This is volume 16 of the Dictionary of Literary Biography series.

369. Dole, Nathan Haskell; Morgan, Forrest; and Ticknor, Caroline. *The Bibliophile Dictionary: A Biographical Record of the Great Authors, with Bibliographical Notices of Their Principal Works from the Beginning of History*. New York; London: International Bibliophile Society, 1904. Reprint. Detroit, MI: Gale Research, 1966.
Originally published as volumes 29 and 30 of the *Bibliophile Library of Literature, Art, and Rare Manuscripts*. Brief biographical data are provided though the style is partly narrative rather than being just a listing of data. Interestingly enough, Nathan Haskell Dole later stated that he "repudiates the use of his name in connection [with this publication]."

370. Wright, Thomas. *Biographia Britannica Literaria; or, Biography of Literary Characters of Great Britain and Ireland, Arranged in Chronological Order*. London: John W. Parker, 1846. Reprint. 2 volumes. Detroit, MI: Gale Research, 1968.
Two volumes provide biobibliographies of British writers of the Anglo-Norman and Anglo-Saxon periods from the fourth through the ninth centuries A.D. A bibliography of anonymous works concludes volume 2, and volume 1 contains a calendar of dates, showing when the profiled writers flourished.

371. Knight, Lucian Lamar. *A Biographical Dictionary of Southern Authors*. Atlanta, GA: Martin & Hoyt Co., 1929. Reprint. Detroit, MI: Gale Research, 1978.
Originally published under the title *The Library of Southern Literature*, Volume XV, *Biographical Dictionary of Authors*, this volume contains approximately 3,800 short sketches on writers from the Southern states. Some include only a name and titles by the individual, while others are much more detailed. Both contemporary writers and those no longer living in the 1920s were included.

372. *A Biographical Dictionary of the Living Authors of Great Britain and Ireland*. London: Henry Colburn, 1816. Reprint. Detroit, MI: Gale Research, 1966.
A collection of biographical sketches on early nineteenth-century British and Irish authors. Each entry includes a short list of writings.

373. Romig, Walter. *The Book of Catholic Authors: Informal Self-Portraits of Famous Catholic Writers*. Volume 1, Detroit, MI: Walter Romig, 1942; Volumes 2 and 3, Grosse Pointe, MI: Walter Romig, 1943 and 1946; reprint ed., Freeport, NY: Books for Libraries Press, 1971.
The biographies of 61 Catholic authors are arranged alphabetically. Each biography includes principle works of the author in addition to several quotations from their works. Many of the biographies are written by themselves.

374. Hopkins, Lee Bennett. *Books Are by People: Interviews with 104 Authors and Illustrators of Books for Young People.* New York: Citation Press, 1969.

    The author interviewed 104 authors and illustrators who have produced books for children from pre-kindergarten through grade 3. In the author group are both established writers and newcomers. Biographies include portraits of the authors and illustrators as well as illustrations from their works. A brief appendix lists Caldecott and Newbery winners.

375. Higgenson, A. Henry. *British and American Sporting Authors: Their Writings and Biographies.* London: Hutchinson & Co. Ltd., 1951.

    Seventeen chapters on authors who have chosen to write on hunting, steeplechasing, and similar sports. Authors range from Edward, Second Duke of York (1373–1415) to Anthony Trollope (1815–82), from Lord North (1836–1933) to people active about the time of this compilation. A few women are included. Emphasis is on the author's contributions and dedication to sporting life rather than biographical data. A lengthy bibliography completes the work.

376. Kunitz, Stanley J., and Haycraft, Howard. *British Authors Before 1800: A Biographical Dictionary.* New York: H. W. Wilson, 1952.

    This alphabetically arranged biographical reference book includes 650 writers. The most pertinent biographical and critical data are included on each subject with a bibliography of principal works at the end of each. Works about the individual are also included. The entries are in narrative form, entertainingly written, and include the basic facts about the subject. This work is intended to be a companion volume for *American Authors: 1600–1900; British Authors of the Nineteenth Century; The Junior Book of Authors;* and *Twentieth Century Authors.*

377. ———. *British Authors of the Nineteenth Century.* New York: H. W. Wilson, 1936.

    There are more than 1,000 entries in this work limited to the British Empire, including Canada, Australia, South Africa, and New Zealand. Authors included must have published the major portion of their work between 1800 and 1900. Preference has been given to writers of *belle lettres*; however, prominent writers in a wide variety of subject areas are included. Citations to works by and about the authors are included in the entries.

378. Weintraub, Stanley. *British Dramatists Since World War II.* 2 volumes. Detroit, MI: Gale Research, 1982.

    Works of 69 dramatists active in Great Britain since World War II are listed, accompanied by essays on each playwright, and including other sources of information about them. Appendices also include relevant essays on the period of activity. This is volume 13 of the Dictionary of Literary Biography series.

379. Staley, Thomas F. *British Novelists 1890–1929: Traditionalists.* Detroit, MI: Gale Research, 1985.

    Thirty-two novelists are covered in essays about them and their works. The entries include lists of their works and other sources about them and their writing. This is volume 34 of the Dictionary of Literary Biography series.

380. Oldsey, Bernard. *British Novelists 1930–1959.* 2 volumes. Detroit, MI: Gale Research, 1983.

Each entry for these 59 novelists includes a listing of his/her works as well as biographical and critical information. Appendices include several interesting essays as well as listings of movies made from their works, prizes won, and further readings. This is volume 15 of the Dictionary of Literary Biography series.

381. Halio, Jay L. *British Novelists Since 1960.* 2 volumes. Detroit, MI: Gale Research, 1983.

In contrast to the volume covering the years 1930-59 which contained 59 entries, these 2 volumes include 107 novelists. A list of the novelist's works is followed by an essay on the writer. Appendices include an essay about the period and a list for further reading. This is volume 14 of the Dictionary of Literary Biography series.

382. Stanford, Donald E. *British Poets 1880–1914.* Detroit, MI: Gale Research, 1983.

Essays, lists of authors' works, and bibliographies of other relevant publications are included in this volume about 43 British poets. This is volume 19 of the Dictionary of Literary Biography series.

383. ———. *British Poets 1914–1945.* Detroit, MI: Gale Research, 1983.

This volume continues where the volume covering 1880–1914 left off and is similar in format. Forty poets were selected for inclusion in the present volume, which covers a period of great political, economic, and social upheaval. Works of the poets, an essay, and a list of other relevant works comprise each biography. This is volume 20 of the Dictionary of Literary Biography series.

384. Scott-Kilvert, Ian. *British Writers.* 8 volumes. New York: Charles Scribner's, 1979.

British Writers complements *American Writers* and came originally from a series of separate articles entitled *Writers and Their Works.* *British Writers* is comprised of a series of articles beginning in the fourteenth century and is arranged in chronological order according to the date of the subject's birth. Each article contains a brief biography and an extensive review of the subject's writings. Also included is a bibliography of works by and about the subject. Each volume includes a chronological table of events with volume 8 consisting of an extensive author, title, and subject index which differentiates between references to biographies and essays.

385. Bailey, Leaonead Pack. *Broadside Authors and Artists: An Illustrated Biographical Directory.* Detroit, MI: Broadside Press, 1974.

This volume provides limited information on 192 Black authors and artists published by Broadside Press who are not usually listed in other biographies. A listing of their published work is part of the entries.

386. Thomas, Clara. *Canadian Novelists 1920–1945. Toronto: Longmans, Green, 1946.*
Provides brief biographies of 122 Canadian novelists, including bibliographies. An appendix groups the authors by broad subject categories.

387. Hoehn, Matthew. *Catholic Authors: Contemporary Biographical Sketches 1930–1947.* 2 volumes. Newark, NJ: St. Mary's Abbey, 1947, 1952.
Over 600 Catholic authors who were living prior to 1930 are represented in brief biographical sketches. Each biography includes a photograph and contains references to the works for which the author is best known. An author list with page references precedes the biographies. The second volume includes 374 "new" authors who were alive at the time or had died since 1930.

388. Sarkissian, Adele. *Children's Authors and Illustrators: An Index to Biographical Dictionaries.* 3d ed. Detroit, MI: Gale Research, 1981.
"*CA & I* aims to include all known writers and illustrators of children's books whose work is accessible in the English language." Some of the authors write for children; the work of others has been adopted by children; and others' works are routinely assigned in classwork. This edition includes 20,000 people with each entry including basic biographical data and abbreviations of reference works containing biographical information on that individual.

389. Spender, Stephen, and Hall, Donald. *The Concise Encyclopedia of English and American Poets and Poetry.* 2d rev. ed. New York: Hawthorn Books, 1970.
A dictionary of literary terms, styles, and people. Arranged alphabetically, short, signed biographical sketches appear among the other entries.

390. Millett, Fred B. *Contemporary American Authors: A Critical Survey and 219 Bio-Bibliographies.* New York: Harcourt, Brace, 1943.
After a lengthy survey of American literature from 1900 to the date of publication, there is an alphabetical listing of 219 authors giving narrative biographical sketches followed by a bibliography of known works by them. The book concludes with a grouping of authors by types, lists of abbreviations of books and periodicals containing studies of them, and an index of authors.

Contemporary Authors (391–94 below) is a set of reference works composed of several different series, all arranged in the same form. The authors profiled in *CA* range from novelists to essayists to prominent scholars. Entries contain a brief biographical headnote, a list of selected works, the author's statement about his/her work, and selected short excerpts from reviews of the author's writings. Selected volumes have cumulative indices to the entire *CA* system.

391. Bryfonski, Dedria. *Contemporary Authors.* Autobiography Series. Detroit, MI: Gale Research, 1984–.
Contemporary writers contributed sketches on other contemporary authors. A bibliography of the author's work is included with each sketch.

392. *Contemporary Authors: A Bio-Bibliographical Guide to Current Authors and Their Works.* First Revision. 107 volumes. Detroit, MI: Gale Research, 1967–83.

This so-called "First Revision" began with a revision of 4 issues of *CA* published in 1962–63. Starting with volume 104, deceased authors whose work was of continuing interest were included. Each volume contains 4 unit numbers until volume 101 when each volume thereafter contains a single number. Cumulative indexes are included periodically in the series.

393. *Contemporary Authors: A Bio-Bibliographical Guide to Current Authors and Their Works.* Permanent Series. 2 volumes. Detroit, MI: Gale Research, 1975–78.

This version of *CA* consists of sketches removed from the ongoing *CA* revision pattern. These sketches represent individuals now deceased or who are no longer actively writing. Each was revised before being included in the Permanent Series.

394. *Contemporary Authors: A Bio-Bibliographical Guide to Current Writers in Fiction, General Nonfiction, Poetry, Journalism, Drama, Motion Pictures, Television, and Other Fields.* New Revision Series. Detroit, MI: Gale Research, 1981–.

With the New Revision series, *CA* began revising and updating only those sketches from previous volumes that needed substantial revision. Thus, sketches from previous volumes in which there had been no change would not be included, and active current writers could be dealt with in a more comprehensive and timely fashion. A "Sidelights" section may include the individual's philosophy, interests, or other personal comments.

395. Vinson, James. *Contemporary Dramatists.* 3d ed. New York: St. Martin's Press, 1982.

Over 300 concise biographies of English-language dramatists, all living at the time of publication. Biographical data are brief, a list of publications follows, and a critical essay concludes each entry. A supplement contained in the same volume provides shorter sketches on 5 groups: screen writers, radio writers, television writers, musical librettists, and theater groups. A title index provides access to information by the titles of a dramatist's work.

396. Borklund, Elmer. *Contemporary Literary Critics.* New York: St. Martin's Press, 1977.

Contemporary Literary Critics emphasizes the work of living and recently deceased critics dealing with Anglo-American literature. Biographical data are short, with a list of the critic's writings, including noncritical works and other biographical materials, as well as a critical essay on the individual's contributions.

397. Vinson, James. *Contemporary Novelists.* 3d ed. New York: St. Martin's Press, 1982.

Each entry includes a biography, a full bibliography, comments by the writer if s/he chose to make any about his/her work, and a critical essay.

398. ———. *Contemporary Poets.* 3d ed. New York: St. Martin's Press, 1980.

Each entry consists of a listing of the standard biographical information, followed by a bibliography of the poet's work, and ending with a critical essay. Many entries also include a commentary on the poet's work if the subject elected to contribute one. Mostly British and American poets are featured, although some others with links to the Commonwealth are also included. In addition, there are entries for 22 poets who have died since 1950 but whose work is contemporary.

399. Reginald, R. *Contemporary Science Fiction Authors.* New York: Arno, 1975.

A biobibliographical dictionary of science fiction and fantasy authors. Bibliographies of 483 authors active during the years 1960–68 and biographies of 308 authors are included; thus, some entries list works but provide no biographical data.

400. *Conversations with Writers.* Detroit, MI: Gale Research, 1977.

Thirteen prominent writers were interviewed, the tapes transcribed, and the transcripts then edited for this work. Insight into how they work and their personality is evident in these interviews. Interviewed were: Vance Bourjaily, James Dickey, William Price Fox, John Gardner, Brendan Gill, Edward Gorey, Robert Hayden, Mary Welsh Hemingway, Ring Lardner, Jr., Wallace Markfield, Donald Ogden Stewart, Thomas Tryon, and Robert Penn Warren.

401. *Conversations with Writers II.* Detroit, MI: Gale Research, 1978.

Eleven writers are interviewed in this book of edited transcripts derived from tapes: Stanley Ellin, James T. Farrell, Irvin Faust, Barbara Ferry Johnson, Roger Kahn, Anita Loos, James A. Michener, James Purdy, Ishmael Reed, William Styron, and Eudora Welty.

402. Allibone, S. Austin. *A Critical Dictionary of English Literature and British and American Authors Living and Deceased from the Earliest Accounts to the Latter Half of the Nineteenth Century.* 3 volumes. Philadelphia, PA: J. B. Lippincott, 1858–97. Reprint of 1858–71 eds. Detroit, MI: Gale Research, 1965. (See also *A Supplement to Allibone's Critical Dictionary....*)

More than 46,000 entries (some extremely brief) are included; longer ones are narrative in style and include quotations. There are 40 topical indexes.

403. Magill, Frank W. *Cyclopedia of World Authors.* Rev. ed. 3 volumes. Englewood Cliffs, NJ: Salem Press, 1974.

Around 1,000 sketches of world authors are included. Basic biographical information and a list of principal works precede each entry; this material is followed by an evaluative narrative about the author and concludes with bibliographical references helpful to the researcher.

404. Adams, Oscar Fay. *A Dictionary of American Authors.* 5th ed. Boston: Houghton Mifflin, 1904. Reprint. Detroit, MI: Gale Research Co., 1969.

A directory of living and deceased writers in the United States. A brief one- or 2-sentence annotation describes each author's career, and a list of works follows.

405. Johnson, Rossiter. *A Dictionary of Biographies of Authors Represented in the Authors Digest Series: With a Supplemental List of Later Titles and a Supplemental Biographical Section.* New York: Authors Press, 1908, 1927. Reprint. Detroit, MI: Gale Research, 1974.

This international biographical work provides sketches on authors as diverse as Cervantes (1547–1616), Turgenyev (1818–83), and Edith Wharton, who was living when the book was published in 1927. Entries provide brief personal data, some critical commentary, and a bibliography of noted works. The supplemental biographies are all on persons living at the time of original publication.

406. Houfe, Simon. *A Dictionary of British Book Illustrators and Caricaturists 1800–1914.* Rev. ed. Woodbridge, Suffolk, England: The Antique Collector's Club, 1981.

A little over half of this volume is devoted to a dictionary of British illustrators. Illustrators are listed alphabetically, and biographical sketches vary in length from one line to several hundred words. Included are lists of works and references to galleries and museums where they reside. Numerous examples of their works appear. The first half of this work is devoted to chapters on history and background, all intended to help the collector.

407. Sharp, Robert Farquharson. *A Dictionary of English Authors, Biographical and Bibliographical.* 2d ed. London: George Redway, 1898.

Covers the "lives and writings of 700 British writers from the year 1400 to the present time." Entries are in a "Who's Who" form, listing factual data, and followed by a list of works.

408. Cleeve, Brian. *Dictionary of Irish Writers.* 3 volumes. Cork, Ireland: Mercier Press, 1967–71.

Short biographical sketches of fiction and nonfiction Irish authors make up this set.

409. Van Antwerp, Margaret A. *Dictionary of Literary Biography Documentary Series: An Illustrated Chronicle.* 4 volumes. Detroit, MI: Gale Research, 1982–84.

This work supplements the Dictionary of Literary Biography volumes. Each volume treats in depth major figures of a particular period, movement, or genre in lengthy essays. Illustrations include photographs and facsimiles.

410. Atkinson, Frank. *Dictionary of Literary Pseudonyms: A Selection of Popular Modern Writers in English.* 2d. ed. Hamden, CT: Linnet Books, 1977.
    Divided into 2 parts, this book lists authors' pen names under their real names and cross-references pen names to real names.

411. Spence, Lewis. *A Dictionary of Medieval Romance and Romance Writers.* London: G. Routledge & Sons, Ltd.; New York: E. P. Dutton, 1913. Reprint. New York: Humanities Press, 1962.
    Most of the entries in this dictionary are devoted to characters and places in medieval fiction, but there is also information about the people who wrote these works. Data are sketchy, as not a great deal of information is available about these writers. Nevertheless, this source could be invaluable to the person researching early western literature.

412. Wallace, W. Stewart. *A Dictionary of North American Authors Deceased Before 1950.* Toronto: Ryerson Press, 1951.
    An alphabetical listing of North Americans who wrote novels or nonfiction and died before 1950. Each entry lists basic data, followed by a code which provides access to the individual's biography in one of 78 biographical references.

413. Staff of Poets and Writers, Inc. *A Directory of American Poets.* New York: Poets and Writers, 1973.
    A directory of 1,300 living poets and writers who have published works in the United States. In addition to his/her address, the directory lists the poet's teaching level, interests, languages spoken, and selected recent titles. The *Directory* is updated by a supplemental publication entitled *Coda: Poets and Writers Newsletter.*

414. *A Directory of American Poets and Fiction Writers.* New York: Poets and Writers, 1983.
    A merger of *A Directory of American Poets* and *Directory of American Fiction Writers.* Provides over 5,000 names and addresses of poets and fiction writers whose work has been published in the United States.

415. Vinson, James. *Dramatists.* New York: St. Martin's Press, 1979.
    More than 125 dramatists are profiled in entries that include biographical data, a bibliography of his/her works, and citations of other sources of information on the author. There is also a critique of the writer's work.

416. Kunitz, Stanley J., and Colby, Vineta. *European Authors 1000–1900: A Biographical Dictionary of European Literature.* New York: H. W. Wilson, 1968.
    Over 900 biocritical essays on authors covering 900 years of Western literature make up the content of this book. Entries are signed and include short bibliographies.

417. Browning, D. C. *Everyman's Dictionary of Literary Biography, English and American.* New York: E. P. Dutton, 1958.
    An alphabetical guide to living and deceased writers of the United States, the British Isles, and some of the British Commonwealth countries. Entries are brief and include vital data as well as a selected list of works.

418. Benet, Laura. *Famous American Poets.* New York: Dodd, Mead, 1950.

Twenty-two American poets are described in this book, which is illustrated and indexed.

419. Coffman, Raymon Peyton, and Goodman, Nathan G. *Famous Author-Illustrators for Young People.* New York: Dodd, Mead, 1943.

This work originally appeared under the title *Famous Authors for Boys and Girls.* Contains biographies of 19 famous authors beginning with William Shakespeare and ending with Jack London.

420. Vinson, James. *Great Writers of the English Language.* See *Poets, Novelists and Prose Writers,* and *Dramatists.*

421. *Index to the Wilson Author Series.* New York: H. W. Wilson, 1976.

This is an index to biographical dictionaries in the series: *American Authors: 1600–1900; British Authors Before 1800; British Authors of the Nineteenth Century; European Authors: 1000–1900; Twentieth Century Authors* and its supplement; and *World Authors: 1950–1970.*

422. Gaster, Adrian. *International Authors and Writers Who's Who.* 9th ed. Cambridge: Melrose Press Ltd., 1982. (See also *International Who's Who in Poetry.*)

The biographies included are for authors currently living; the countries covered represent virtually the entire world. Authors must have produced more than one work, and no attempt has been made to include authors of pamphlets or works of a highly technical nature. There are approximately 6,000 entries. Unfortunately, for ease of access, this has been bound with *International Who's Who in Poetry.*

423. Kay, Ernest. *International Who's Who in Poetry.* 6th ed. Cambridge: Melrose Press, 1982. (See also *International Authors and Writers Who's Who.*)

This sixth edition of the poetry *Who's Who* is bound with the ninth edition of the *Authors and Writers Who's Who,* thus making the poetry volume inaccessible, as it is hidden in the combined volume. Includes approximately 6,000 poets worldwide.

424. Kunitz, Stanley J., and Haycraft, Howard. *The Junior Book of Authors.* 2d rev. ed. New York: H. W. Wilson, 1951.

Presents short biographical or autobiographical sketches of 289 authors of children's literature. Many include a portrait and a short description of the author's works following the biography. Most are English-language authors, but some writers of other nationalities (mostly those whose works have been translated into English) are also included.

425. Untermeyer, Louis. *Lives of the Poets: The Story of One Thousand Years of English and American Poetry.* New York: Simon and Schuster, 1959.

Traces English-language poetry from its roots in the oral tradition through the "age of anxiety" of the mid-twentieth century via biocriticisms of representative poets. An index provides access to names and titles of poems.

426. Weintraub, Stanley. *Modern British Dramatists 1900–1945.* 2
volumes. Detroit, MI: Gale Research, 1982.
>Entries for 73 active dramatists include lists of works of the dramatists,
>an essay, and a selective bibliography. Appendices include essays relevant
>to the activity of the period. This is volume 10 of the Dictionary of
>Literary Biography series.

427. Hopkins, Lee Bennett. *More Books by More People: Interviews
with Sixty-Five Authors of Books for Children.* New York: Citation
Press, 1974.
>Follows the same format as *Books Are by People*, 1969; these are biog-
>raphies created from interviews.

428. Fuller, Muriel. *More Junior Authors.* New York: H. W. Wilson,
1963.
>This companion volume to *Junior Book of Authors* includes biographical
>sketches of children's authors whose works were popular in the 1950s to
>early 1960s. More than 250 authors are included; some sketches are
>autobiographical. A short list of each person's work is included.

429. Kaye, Phyllis Johnson. *National Playwrights Directory.* 2d ed.
Waterford, CT: Eugene O'Neill Theatre Center, 1981.
>A directory of currently active American playwrights, with a résumé of
>their works listed. Most entries include a photograph and some brief
>biographical information. A title index provides cross-references to play-
>wrights' names.

430. Vinson, James. *Novelists and Prose Writers.* New York: St.
Martin's Press, 1979.
>Around 500 writers are profiled in entries that include biographical data,
>a bibliography of each subject's works, and citations to other sources of
>information on the author. There is also a critique of the author's work.

431. Seymour-Smith, Martin. *Novels and Novelists: A Guide to the
World of Fiction.* New York: St. Martin's Press, 1980.
>An encyclopedic history of fiction from ancient mythology to the 1970s.
>A chapter entitled "Novelists: An Alphabetical Guide" includes a brief
>description of each author's work and includes a list of up to 3 works by
>the person, each rated on readability, characterization, plot, and literary
>merit.

432. Coyle, William. *Ohio Authors and Their Books: Biographical
Data and Selective Bibliographies for Ohio Authors, Native and
Resident, 1796–1950.* Cleveland, OH: World Publishing, 1962.
>Contains biobibliographies of Ohio's authors, including native Ohioans
>and those born elsewhere, who wrote while residing in the Buckeye State.

433. Nicholson, Margaret E. *People in Books: A Selective Guide to
Biographical Literature Arranged by Vocation and Other Fields of
Reader Interest.* New York: H. W. Wilson, 1969.
>An index by subject to biographies that might be of interest to children
>or young adult library patrons. The subject entries are actually career or
>profession designations, and several indexes at the back of the book
>provide alternative access points, such as by country, then century, or by

surname. Autobiographies are listed in another appendix, and there is a list of publishers' and distributors' addresses.

Sufficient bibliographic information is supplied with each entry to allow patrons to locate, or even order, a title. Despite its young adult-intended audience, *People in Books* could be a useful source for adult collections or college libraries as well.

434. Vinson, James. *Poets.* New York: St. Martin's Press, 1979.
Five hundred poets are profiled in entries that include biographical data, a bibliography of the subject's works, and citations of other sources of information on the author. There is also a critique of the poet's work.

435. Hamilton, Walter. *The Poets Laureate of England. Being a History of the Office of Poet Laureate, Biographical Notices of Its Holders, and a Collection of the Satires, Epigrams, and Lampoons Directed Against Them.* London: Elliott Stock, 1879. Reprint. Detroit, MI: Gale Research, 1968.
This work covers poets laureate from Geoffrey Chaucer to Alfred Tennyson. Includes a chronological chart listing them. Early laureates were volunteers rather than official appointees. Discusses their problems, their career, their style.

436. Sherry, Vincent B., Jr. *Poets of Great Britain and Ireland 1945–1960.* Detroit, MI: Gale Research, 1984.
Contains 44 essays on important poets active during this post-war period, preceded by selected publications and followed by selected sources. This is volume 27 of the Dictionary of Literary Biography series.

437. O'Donoghue, D. J. *The Poets of Ireland: A Biographical and Bibliographical Dictionary of Irish Writers of English Verse.* London: Oxford University Press, 1912. Reprint. Detroit, MI: Gale Research, 1968.
Confined to Irish men and women who used the English language. Entries are brief bibliographical listings by author with biographical information supplied when available.

438. Haynes, John Edward. *Pseudonyms of Authors, Including Anonyms and Initialisms.* New York: John Edward Haynes, 1882. Reprint. Detroit, MI: Gale Research, 1969.
An alphabetical list of authors' pseudonyms, with the author's given name and birth and death dates listed next to the pen name.

439. Commire, Anne. *Something about the Author: Facts and Pictures about Authors and Illustrators of Books for Young People.* 41 volumes. Detroit, MI: Gale Research, 1971–. (Volumes 21–41 were issued in 1985.)
A children's authors' version of *Contemporary Authors,* this set of volumes includes personal and career information, a list of writings, and a few quotations by the author. Most entries have a photograph, and many have selected illustrations from the authors' publications. Includes cumulative author and illustration indexes.

440. Bain, Robert; Flora, Joseph M.; and Rubin, Louis D., Jr.
Southern Writers: A Biographical Dictionary. Baton Rouge, LA:
Louisiana State University Press, 1979.
 More than 379 authors considered "Southern writers" are included in
 this compilation, a project of the Society for the Study of Southern
 Literature. Dozens of scholars wrote the signed essays, which consist of
 entries containing basic biographical data, followed by a narrative on the
 author, and concluding with bibliographical information on the author's
 works.

441. Kirk, John Foster. *A Supplement to Allibone's Critical Dictionary
of English Literature and British and American Authors.* Philadephia,
PA: J. B. Lippincott & Co., 1891. Reprint. 2 volumes. Detroit, MI:
Gale Research, 1965. (See also *Allibone's Critical Dictionary of
English Literature and British and American Authors....*)
 Contains 37,000 entries from periods that were not covered by Allibone's
 original work. Entries consist of brief biographical data, though some are
 in narrative form.

442. MacNicholas, John. *Twentieth-Century American Dramatists.* 2
volumes. Detroit, MI: Gale Research, 1981.
 Seventy-eight American dramatists are featured. Works of each dramatist
 are listed, followed by an essay on him/her, with a listing of other
 relevant research materials completing the entries. Appendices include:
 Trends in Theatrical Productions, Major Regional Theatres, and Books
 for Further Reading. This is volume 7 of the Dictionary of Literary
 Biography series.

443. Wilson, Clyde N. *Twentieth-Century American Historians.*
Detroit, MI: Gale Research, 1983.
 Each entry for the 59 writers contains a list of the historian's works, an
 essay on the person, and a list of additional readings. There is also a
 supplementary list of relevant works. This is volume 17 of the Dictionary
 of Literary Biography series.

444. Cowart, David, and Wymer, Thomas L. *Twentieth-Century
American Science-Fiction Writers.* 2 volumes. Detroit, MI: Gale
Research, 1981.
 Coverage is of 91 science fiction authors active in the first 70 years of the
 twentieth century. The works of each author are listed, plus an essay on
 him/her and a list of additional relevant research materials. An appendix
 lists science fiction works published during the years 1818–1979. This is
 volume 8 of the Dictionary of Literary Biography series.

445. McNeil, Barbara. *Twentieth-Century Author Biographies Master
Index: A Consolidated Index to More than 170,000 Biographical
Sketches concerning Modern Day Authors as They Appear in a
Selection of the Principal Biographical Dictionaries Devoted to
Authors, Poets, Journalists, and Other Literary Figures.* Detroit, MI:
Gale Research, 1984.
 As the title indicates, this volume provides access to biographical in-
 formation on twentieth-century writers.

446. Kunitz, Stanley, and Haycraft, Howard. *Twentieth Century Authors: A Biographical Dictionary of Modern Literature.* Bronx, NY: H. W. Wilson, 1942.

Provides biographical sketches of authors, regardless of nationality, whose works "are familiar to readers of English." Foreign authors are included when translations of their works have gained acceptance in the United States and Great Britain. Entries include a list of works, career development, and a portrait, if available.

447. Kirkpatrick, D. L. *Twentieth Century Children's Writers.* New York: St. Martin's Press, 1983.

Approximately 700 children's authors are included in this second edition of a major resource for researchers working in this literary area. About 100 are new additions to the work; those entries that appeared in the 1978 edition have been revised.

The alphabetically arranged entries provide a biography, an essay critiquing the writer's body of work, and a bibliography. Of interest to researchers will be the appendix of nineteenth-century authors who are considered influential to the productive era of twentieth-century children's literature. Similarly, foreign writers of influence are also identified.

448. Reilly, John M. *Twentieth-Century Crime and Mystery Writers.* New York: St. Martin's Press, 1980.

Includes entries on genre writers, including checklists of authors' works. Some minor writers are included with major ones excluded or only covered briefly.

449. Vinson, James. *Twentieth Century Romance and Gothic Writers.* Detroit, MI: Gale Research, 1982.

More than 300 romance and gothic writers are included in this compilation. A typical entry consists of a brief biography listing the birth and death dates, real name of the writer, education, occupation, and any other pertinent facts such as honors received.

Following that vita is a listing of the writer's works. Finally, there is a signed essay on the career and writing style of the writer, highlighting any events that affected the author's writing. A title index lists all the works cited in this reference. Also included is a bibliography of works about the genre.

450. Smith, Curtis C. *Twentieth-Century Science-Fiction Writers.* New York: St. Martin's Press, 1981.

Approximately 600 English-language science fiction authors active from 1895 to the time of publication are profiled in signed essays. Biographical and bibliographical data are included; the essays are evaluative in tone. There is also a lengthy reading list to aid users in finding more information on the genre, an introduction to the genre, and a list of writers who qualify for this designation.

451. Vinson, James. *Twentieth Century Western Writers*. Detroit, MI: Gale Research, 1982.
> The biographies of more than 300 writers of Western fiction comprise the contents of this work. A short résumé of each writer's career precedes a survey of his/her work. A signed critical essay concludes each entry.

452. Nadel, Ira B., and Fredeman, William E. *Victorian Novelists After 1885*. Detroit, MI: Gale Research, 1983.
> Thirty-nine Victorian novelists are included. Essays describe their careers and work. Publications by the writers are included as well as a bibliography of other sources. This is volume 18 of the Dictionary of Literary Biography Series.

453. ———. *Victorian Novelists Before 1885*. Detroit, MI: Gale Research, 1983.
> Thirty Victorians, all British, are included in the essays and bibliographies of author's works as well as other research sources that have become characteristic of entries in the Dictionary of Literary Biography. There are also 7 reprinted articles. This is volume 21 of the Dictionary of Literary Biography series.

454. Fredeman, William E., and Nadel, Ira B. *Victorian Poets After 1850*. Detroit, MI: Gale Research, 1985.
> Includes 41 entries beginning with William Allingham and ending with Thomas Woolner. Also included are 2 appendices: one that contains essays about the aesthetic concerns of the late Victorian period and another that contains documents relating to the major issues of the Pre-Raphaelite controversy. Also included is a short bibliography for further reading. This is volume 35 of the Dictionary of Literary Biography series.

455. ———. *Victorian Poets Before 1850*. Detroit, MI: Gale Research, 1984.
> This volume includes 41 entries beginning with Matthew Arnold and ending with Isaac Williams. Included in the appendix are several essays describing the Victorian Age. There is a bibliography listing titles for further reading. This is volume 32 of the Dictionary of Literary Biography series.

456. *Who Was Who among English and European Authors 1931–1949*. 3 volumes. Detroit, MI: Gale Research, 1978.
> Approximately 23,000 entries, not all of which are complete, list very basic biographical data. Many famous authors are omitted or receive short shrift.

457. *Who Was Who among North American Authors 1921–1939*. 2 volumes. Detroit, MI: Gale Research, 1976.
> An update of the 7-volume series *Who's Who among North American Writers*, by Alberta Lawrence (Los Angeles: Golden Syndicate, 1921–39), this work includes biographical data on authors ranging from chemists to educators to professional novelists.

458. *Who Was Who in American History: Arts and Letters.* Chicago: Marquis Who's Who, 1975.
About 10,000 biographical sketches of deceased artists, performers, and writers from 1607 to mid-1973 are included in this work.

459. *Who Was Who in Literature, 1906–1934.* 2 volumes. Detroit, MI: Gale Research, 1979.
A lengthy subtitle describes the contents of this set: "based on entries that appeared in *Literary Yearbook* (1906–13), *Literary Yearbook and Author's Who's Who* (1914–17), *Literary Yearbook* (1920–22), and *Who's Who in Literature* (1924–34)." There are 10,400 entries, each consisting of the author's name, titles or degrees held by that person, a list of publications, and a current address. If the subject had died before publication of the work, the date of death is listed.

460. Doyle, Brian. *Who's Who of Children's Literature.* New York: Schocken Books, 1968.
A biographical dictionary of the authors and illustrators of the best known English-language children's books. Both living and deceased authors and illustrators are included; examples of the illustrators' work appear throughout the book. A list of Carnegie (British) and Caldecott and Newbery award winners through 1967 is included, as is an extensive bibliography.

461. Gaines, James R. *Wit's End: Days and Nights of the Algonquin Round Table.* New York: Harcourt Brace Jovanovich, 1977.
A history of the famous 1920s-era literary circle, emphasizing its 10 central figures and 9 others who participated in it. Emphasis is on the group's development as a cultural emblem of its time, although individual members are treated as separate identities.

462. Wakeman, John. *World Authors 1950–1970: A Companion Volume to Twentieth Century Authors.* New York: H. W. Wilson, 1975.
An international guide to authors publishing during the 20-year span of 1950–70. Photographic portraits accompany many of the sketches, which feature interviews with the authors (when possible) and criticism of the individual's work. A short bibliography of principal works by and about the author concludes each sketch.

463. ———. *World Authors 1970–1975.* New York: H. W. Wilson, 1980.
This companion to *Twentieth Century Authors* and *World Authors 1950–1970* contains biocritical essays on individuals who were not profiled in other volumes of the series or who gained prominence in the period 1970–75. Bibliographies of works by and about the author follow each essay, and portraits are included with most of them.

464. Colby, Vineta. *World Authors 1975–1980.* New York: H. W. Wilson, 1985.
This work profiles 379 writers, with about one-third of the entries containing contributions or statements from the authors themselves. The writers are ones who came to prominence during this period. Entries are

critical and biographical in nature, include a listing of prominent works, and indicate where additional information can be found.

465. *The Writers Directory.* 5th ed. Detroit, MI: Gale Research, 1981. Biennial.

A "Who's Who"-type directory of English-language authors, *The Writers Directory* provides brief information about 15,000 fiction and nonfiction writers, dramatists, and poets. Entries include career and educational background, a list of publications, dates, and addresses. Much of the information is provided by the authors themselves or their publishing houses. Only living persons are included. A "Yellow Pages" section at the back indexes authors by writing categories and subjects.

466. Sarkissian, Adele. *Writers for Young Adults: Biographies Master Index: An Index to Sources of Biographical Information.* 2d ed. Detroit, MI: Gale Research, 1984.

It can be frustrating to try to find biographical data on the many authors who concentrate on writing for young adults. This index provides the locations of biographies for 15,000 authors appearing in 500 sources. Similar to *Biography and Genealogy Master Index* in concept and format.

467. Commire, Anne. *Yesterday's Authors of Books for Children.* 2 volumes. Detroit, MI: Gale Research, 1977–78.

Provides biographical information on children's authors who died prior to 1961. Included with the biographies are portraits of the authors and representative illustrations from their books. Each volume contains some 40 biographies.

XIII. The Arts

GENERAL

468. Kronenberger, Louis. *Atlantic Brief Lives: A Biographical Companion to the Arts.* Boston: Little, Brown & Co., 1971.
Over 1,000 people are subjects of biographies in this book; 211 are discussed in lengthy essays. Brief biographical data are provided for the individuals not covered in essays. Arrangement is alphabetical and covers people important in the literature, arts, and music of the Western World. A bibliography follows most entries.

469. McNeil, Barbara, and Herbert, Miranda C. *Performing Arts Biography Master Index: A Consolidated Index to Over 270,000 Biographical Sketches of Persons Living and Dead as They Appear in Over 100 of the Principal Biographical Dictionaries Devoted to the Performing Arts.* 2d ed. Detroit, MI: Gale Research, 1981.
Each entry includes the name, life dates, and sources of biographical information on the individual. Full bibliographical information is given for the sources indexed.

ARCHITECTURE AND ARCHITECTS

470. Gane, John F. *American Architects Directory.* 3d ed. New York: R. R. Bowker, 1970.
More than 23,000 architects are included in this directory. Brief biographical data are given for many; for others, only the name and address are supplied. There is also a geographical index.

471. Withey, Henry F., and Withey, Elsie Rathburn. *Biographical Dictionary of American Architects, Deceased.* Los Angeles: Hennessey & Ingalls, Inc., 1970.
Two thousand men and women and their lives and achievements are included in brief narrative profiles for the period of about 1740 to 1952.

472. Colvin, Howard Montagu. *A Biographical Dictionary of British Architects, 1600–1840.* Rev. and enlarged ed. New York: Facts on File, 1980.
Biographical sketches are provided on architects practicing in England, Scotland, and Wales during this period. The architects' significant works are listed chronologically. Indexes for buildings and names provide access.

473. Emanuel, Muriel. *Contemporary Architects.* London: Macmillan Press Ltd., 1980.
The term "architect" is interpreted loosely in this work. Emphasizing those still living or recently deceased, building designers are profiled along with influential planners and theorists, as well as landscape architects and structural engineers. Architects of the modern movement who did work from the 1920s into the 1950s that still exerts influence over current works are covered as well as those still working in 1980.

These profiles emphasize the professional careers and contributions of selected artists. Entries include basic personal information, lists of well-known designs or influential buildings, a statement of the architect's philosophy, and an analysis of his/her work by fellow architects or architectural critics; publications about the designer are listed in a short bibliography.

474. Placzek, Adolf K. *Macmillan Encyclopedia of Architects.* 4 volumes. New York: Free Press/Macmillan, 1982.
Approximately 2,400 deceased and living architects born prior to the end of 1930 are included. The essays are biographical and bibliographical in nature and are written by authorities on the individuals. A list of each architect's works is also included. A glossary will assist the layperson using this work. Indices include a name index and an index of architectural works alluded to in this encyclopedia. A chronological list of those profiled is provided in a general bibliography to additional information.

475. Peter, John. *Masters of Modern Architecture.* New York: George Brazilier, Inc., 1958.
This work consists primarily of photographs of architectural works. However, included in the appendix are 65 very brief biographies for well-known modern architects.

476. Richards, J. M. *Who's Who in Architecture from 1400 to the Present.* New York: Holt, Rinehart and Winston, 1977.
Beginning with the Italian Renaissance, when the concept of professional building design began, and continuing through the late 1970s, this work covers the Western World, including Europe and the Americas, plus modern Japan, Israel, and the British Commonwealth. The book includes living as well as deceased architects, and photos of their work are included whenever possible. More than 600 architects are profiled. Also included are prominent amateur architects such as Thomas Jefferson.

MUSIC AND MUSICIANS

477. Ewen, David. *American Composers: A Biographical Dictionary.* New York: Putnam, 1982.
>The coverage period is from the Colonial period to the present; 300 composers are included. Each entry includes biographical data; a description of the composer's style, achievements, and principal works; and a selective bibliography. A part of each entry is a section either written by the composer or extracted from writings by or about the composer and is intended to reveal the feelings and intent of the composer in his/her approach to music.

478. Balliet, Whitney. *American Singers.* New York: Oxford University Press, 1979.
>A history of twentieth-century popular singing, emphasizing particular styles and types through exemplary performers. The chapter-length sketches are gossipy and stress each singer's career more than his/her entire life.

479. *The ASCAP Biographical Dictionary of Composers, Authors and Publishers.* 4th ed. New York: R. R. Bowker, 1980.
>Contains more than 8,000 entries of standard biographical data on a portion of the ASCAP (American Society of Composers, Authors, and Publishers) membership. There is also a listing of 7,000 members who are publishers.

480. Slonimsky, Nicolas. *Baker's Biographical Dictionary of Musicians.* 7th ed. New York: Schirmer Books, 1984.
>First published in 1900, Baker's is an example of a well-respected reference book. The usual biographical information on living and dead musicians is included along with lists of works. Some bibliographical data are also included. "Musician" here means not only the performers and creators but also other personnel in the music world such as instructors and critics.

481. Claghorn, Charles Eugene. *Biographical Dictionary of American Music.* West Nyack, NY: Parker Publishing Co., Inc., 1973.
>Over 5,000 musicians who were born in the U.S. or lived in America for a long period of time are included. Coverage extends from the seventeenth century to the time of publication, so most of American history is covered. Entries are brief, but awards and major compositions or career achievements are included with the basic biographical data.

482. ———. *Biographical Dictionary of Jazz.* Englewood Cliffs, NJ: Prentice-Hall, 1982.
>An alphabetical arrangement that includes basic biographical data, musician's specialty, quotations from album covers, articles, obituaries, and other published sources. Entries are concise. An index of groups is also included.

483. Harris, Sheldon. *Blues Who's Who: A Biographical Dictionary of Blues Singers.* New Rochelle, NY: Arlington House, 1979.
Of particular value in this work are the listings of performances by the individuals included and their real and adopted names. The usual biographical information is included as well as instruments played, compositions, accounts of their careers, and references for additional information.

484. Kallman, Helmut. *Catalogue of Canadian Composers.* Rev. and enl. ed. N.P.: Canadian Broadcasting Corporation, 1952.
In addition to other information about the status of musical composition in mid-twentieth-century Canada, this work contains brief biographies of living and deceased Canadian composers and a list of their works.

485. Ewen, David. *Composers of Tomorrow's Music: A Non-Technical Introduction to the Musical and Avant-Garde Movement.* New York: Dodd, Mead & Co., 1971.
Chapter-length biocritical essays on 10 composers who have specialized in avant-garde composition.

486. ———. *Composers of Yesterday: A Biographical and Critical Guide to the Most Important Composers of the Past.* New York: H. W. Wilson, 1937.
Sketches on deceased composers comprise this volume. The editor/compiler states that his purpose is to satisfy the music lover's curiosity about well-loved composers. Personal details are included with each person's career history, and there is information about critical response to the person's compositions. Lists of principal works, other biographical sources, and a discography conclude each entry, many of which include portraits.

487. ———. *Composers Since 1900: A Biographical and Critical Guide.* New York: H. W. Wilson, 1969 with supplement.
Composers Since 1900 provides biographies of Western composers (Europe, the Americas, and Australia). Europeans dominate the work with selection of composers being based on the importance of the artist's work, the frequency with which it is performed, and the overall interest aroused by the artist and his/her work. Excluded were composers generating only local or passing interest or whose work is not generally available. Personal data are included, but the emphasis is on the artist's career: with whom s/he studied, notable performances, posts held, and awards won. Critics' appraisal of the person's compositions complete the entries. At the end of each entry is a list of works by type, e.g., ballets, chamber music, choral works, etc., and a bibliography of other writings about the composer.

488. Kutsch, K.J., and Riemens, Leo. Translated from the German, Expanded and Annotated by Harry Earl Jones. *A Concise Biographical Dictionary of Singers from the Beginning of Recorded Sound to the Present.* Philadelphia, PA: Chilton Book Co., 1969.
Emphasizing performers of opera, operettas, and the art-song, this work profiles Western singers of the twentieth century. Entries include personal and professional data, as well as a short discography.

489. Anderson, E. Ruth. *Contemporary American Composers: A Biographical Dictionary.* 2d ed. Boston: G. K. Hall, 1982.

Composers born since 1870, and those of American citizenship (or extended residence in the United States), are eligible for inclusion in this biographical dictionary. Those writing only teaching pieces, jazz, popular, rock, or folk music are excluded. Living subjects of profiles completed questionnaires for this work, and the information supplied was accepted with "a minimum of verification." Vital information on life dates, educational background, awards, and lists of works is provided in short sketches.

490. *Conversations with Jazz Musicians.* Detroit, MI: Gale, 1977.

Eleven major jazz musicians are interviewed: Louis Bellson, Leon Breeden, Dizzy Gillespie, Eric Kloss, Jimmy McPartland, Barry Miles, Sy Oliver, Charlie Spivak, Betty Taylor, Phil Woods, and Sol Yaged. All interviews were done by Zane Knauss.

491. Butterworth, Neil. *A Dictionary of American Composers.* New York: Garland, 1984.

Over 500 "serious" composers are included in entries that combine facts with narrative. Since the emphasis is on the serious composers who have worked in America since the eighteenth century, many of the well-known composers who are virtually household names, such as Irving Berlin and Cole Porter, are omitted. Important teachers are listed, along with their pupils, in an appendix.

492. Osborne, Charles. *The Dictionary of Composers.* London: Bodley Head, 1977.

Biographical essays describe the careers of composers. The primary criterion for inclusion is whether one frequently encounters these composers in performance. The work is intended for ready reference use by avid music enthusiasts.

493. Gilder, Eric, and Port, June G. *Dictionary of Composers and Their Music: Every Listener's Guide.* New York: Facts on File, 1978.

This book helps music enthusiasts determine who wrote what and when. Composers of works heard in the concert hall, opera or ballet house, or church are listed here, with their vital dates and a chronological listing of their compositions. Composers range from Thomas Tallis, who was born in the very early sixteenth century, to the present.

494. Eaglefield-Hull, A. *A Dictionary of Modern Music and Musicians.* New York: E. P. Dutton, 1924. Reprint. New York: Da Capo Press, 1971.

Music terminology and musicians' biographies are mingled in this guide to late nineteenth- and early twentieth-century composers. A list of writings and compositions follows the appropriate entries.

495. Stambler, Irwin, and Landon, Grelun. *The Encyclopedia of Folk, Country and Western Music.* 2d ed. New York: St. Martin's Press, 1984.

Biographies of American folk and country-and-western musicians appear throughout this dictionary-arrangement encyclopedia. Rural blues performers are included. Entries contain personal data, a chronicle of the musician's career, and some critical analysis. Well-known musical bands and groups are also profiled here.

496. Gerig, Reginald R. *Famous Pianists and Their Technique.* Washington, DC: Robert B. Luce, Inc., 1974.
This work traces the development of various piano techniques through the history of keyboard playing. Arranged into chapters by technical style, most styles are linked with one of 2 major interpreters, such as Czerny, Chopin, or Liszt. A bibliography, glossary, and index provide access to names in this book and other sources of information.

497. Lahee, Henry Charles. *Famous Singers of To-Day and Yesterday.* New York: L. C. Page, 1898. Reprint. Boston: Longwood Press, 1878.
A history of noteworthy opera performers, from 1600 to the late nineteenth century. An overview of singing from 1600 to 1800 opens the book, and subsequent chapters address nineteenth-century opera by chronological period. Biographical information centers on each singer's career more than on the person's private life. There is also a lengthy "Chronological Table of Famous Singers" that includes each performers' dates of birth, debut, retirement, and death.

498. Feather, Leonard. *From Satchmo to Miles.* New York: Stein and Day, 1972.
This volume contains a series of 13 biocritical sketches on modern jazz artists by one of the best-known jazz critics. In addition to the artists cited in the title, the following are profiled: Duke Ellington, Billie Holiday, Ella Fitzgerald, Count Basie, Lester Young, Charlie Parker, Dizzy Gillespie, Norman Granz, Oscar Peterson, Ray Charles, and Don Ellis.

499. Terkel, Studs. *Giants of Jazz.* Rev. ed. New York: Thomas Y. Crowell Co., 1975.
Presents 14 biographies of American jazz greats, arranged chronologically beginning with King Oliver and concluding with John Coltrane. A discography provides an excellent listing of selected recordings.

500. Pleasants, Henry. *The Great American Popular Singers.* New York: Simon and Schuster, 1974.
Consists of 22 chapter-length biographies devoted to twentieth-century American pop singers. Ranging from jazz to Broadway, country-and-western to gospel, many of the really great names in popular singing are profiled. Numerous photographs illustrate the work, which also includes a glossary of musical terminology and a detailed index.

501. Ewen, David. *Great Composers 1300–1900: A Biographical and Critical Guide.* New York: H. W. Wilson, 1966.
An alphabetical listing of great Western composers, sketches in this volume trace each artist's training and development in music. Portraits appear with most sketches, and a chronological listing of the composers' names follows the dictionary portion, as does a listing of their names by nationality.

502. Zoff, Otto. *Great Composers Through the Eyes of Their Contemporaries.* New York: E.P. Dutton and Co., 1951.
Profiles of 24 famous symphonic composers, based on accounts of their contemporaries and colleagues. Arranged chronologically, essays address musicians from Henry Purcell to George Gershwin. Notes at the end of the book clarify terms and references in the essays, and a list of sources refers the user to other materials about both the composer and those remembering him.

503. Collier, James Lincoln. *The Great Jazz Artists.* New York: Four Winds Press, 1977.
Traces the development of jazz from its roots in Afro-American blues music through the 1960s saxophone work of John Coltrane. This juvenile book focuses on specific musicians to exemplify different periods in the development of the jazz idiom. [Juvenile]

504. Schonberg, Harold C. *The Great Pianists.* New York: Simon and Schuster, 1963.
Biographies of great pianists from the 1770s to the 1960s. Organized into chapters by interpretive style, the book is filled with portraits of the men profiled. There is an index of names; pianists' names include place and date of birth and death.

505. Mach, Elyse. *Great Pianists Speak for Themselves.* New York: Dodd, Mead and Co., 1980.
Contains 13 chapter-length interviews with contemporary Western pianists who have achieved legendary status. Each chapter opens with a short description of the pianist, his/her demeanor and surroundings, and then turns to the artist's own words.

506. Pleasants, Henry. *The Great Singers: From the Dawn of Opera to Our Own Time.* New York: Simon and Schuster, 1966.
A history of opera as manifested by its performers. Opening with a brief discussion of operatic form, the book continues chronologically into the twentieth century. A 5-page glossary of operatic terms assists novice readers, and a bibliography directs them to additional sources.

507. Campbell, Margaret. *The Great Violinists.* Garden City, NY: Doubleday and Co., 1981.
Traces the careers of the great violinists, from Thomas Baltzar, a seventeenth-century virtuoso, to Itzhak Perlman in the late 1970s. Emphasis is placed on the genealogy of technique; a "tree" of "Teacher-pupil Relationships to the Present Day" illustrates this concept. Biographies are treated within the text of chapters addressing style and technique over time. A bibliography and extensive discography offer access to other works, and a detailed index provides references to individual names in the text.

508. Bie, Oscar. Translated by E. E. Kellett and E. W. Naylor. *A History of the Pianoforte and Pianoforte Players.* New York: E. P. Dutton, 1899. Reprint. New York: Da Capo Press, 1968.
Translated freely from a German classic entitled *Das Klavier*, this book traces the musical and geographic history of the piano. Biographical treatment is granted to Scarlatti, Bach, Bach's descendants, Handel,

Hayden, Mozart, Beethoven, the Romantics, and late nineteenth-century "moderns."

509. Bull, Storm. *Index to Biographies of Contemporary Composers.* New York: Scarecrow Press, 1964.

Indexes biographical entries in 67 internationally published reference works containing information about composers who were "still alive [in 1964] or were born in 1900 or later, or died in 1950 or later."

510. Gaster, Adrian. *International Who's Who in Music and Musicians Directory.* 9th ed. Cambridge: Melrose Press; distributed by Gale Research, 1980.

More than 100,000 musicians are included in this compilation. Biographees contributed to the copy. Entries are standard factual biographical format and include performances, roles played, and orchestras of which performers are a part. The appendices list addresses of orchestras, music organizations, major competitions and awards, music libraries, conservatories of music, and Masters of the King's/Queen's Musick (an honorary position in England).

511. Goldberg, Joe. *Jazz Masters of the Fifties.* New York: Macmillan, 1965.

Biographies of the cool jazz and bebop performers who revolutionized American jazz in the 1950s. Twelve chapters profile saxophone, horn, piano, and bass players of the post-World War II era. There are no illustrations or indexes, but each chapter includes a selected discography.

512. Gitler, Ira. *Jazz Masters of the Forties.* New York: Macmillan, 1966.

This work consists of 9 chapter-length biographies, each of which focuses on a particular instrumentalist. In each chapter, the author refers to dozens of additional musicians, requiring the reader to refer to the name index in order to locate particular individuals. Each chapter concludes with a short discography.

513. Hadlock, Richard. *Jazz Masters of the Twenties.* New York: Macmillan, 1965.

Chronicles the development of the American jazz idiom during the 20s via the work of its best performers. One chapter is devoted to "The Chicagoans," the group of individually less famous but collectively influential jazz players from the Windy City. Each chapter closes with a short list of recommended readings and recordings.

514. Rasponi, Lanfranco. *The Last Prima Donnas.* New York: Alfred A. Knopf, 1982.

An opera buff's guide to the great female voices of the past. Rasponi included only those divas who are deceased and whom he had interviewed sometime from the 1930s to 1980. He chose selectively women who "either excelled in a certain repertoire or in a certain style of singing, or achieved a position of pre-eminence for a number of different reasons." Using his selection criteria to organize the book, Rasponi categorizes them into 18 chapters, ranging from "The Huge Voices" to "The Money Makers."

515. Roxon, Lillian. *Lillian Roxon's Rock Encyclopedia.* New York: Grosset and Dunlap, 1969.

Individuals seeking biographical information on rock performers and groups through the 1960s would do well to look here. A list of recordings, both albums and singles, follows each profile. Appendices list the *Cash Box* top albums for 1960–68 and *Billboard*'s Number 1 weekly hits for 1950 through 1967.

516. Schonberg, Harold C. *The Lives of the Great Composers.* Rev. ed. New York: W. W. Norton & Co., 1981.

Chronologically traces Western symphonic composition in a series of biographical essays beginning with Claudio Monteverdi. Lives and works of 2 or 3 composers are often compared within the chapters.

517. Thomas, Henry, and Thomas, Dana Lee. *Living Biographies of the Great Composers.* New York: Garden City Publishing Co., Inc., 1940.

Biographies of 20 great composers of Western symphonic music are included. Contrary to the title's implication, these are not biographies of composers alive in 1940. Those profiled begin with Bach and continue to Stravinsky. Each essay includes a highly selective list of "Great Compositions," a pen-and-ink portrait, and a biography of the composer's life and career.

518. Ewen, David. *Living Musicians.* New York: H. W. Wilson, 1940, with supplement.

A book of representative major musicians living in the mid-twentieth century. The individual's musical career is emphasized, and some critical analysis accompanies the entries. "Biographies" of famous musical ensembles are included as well. A classified list of musicians by specialty (vocal range or instrument) concludes the volume.

519. Wolff, Konrad. *Masters of the Keyboard: Individual Style Elements in the Piano Music of Bach, Haydn, Mozart, Beethoven, and Schubert.* Bloomington, IN: Indiana University Press, 1983.

Devoted to the development of keyboard style by the most famous Western piano composers, this work avoids traditional study of the subject's life and focuses instead on his/her musical and technical development and influence. A bibliography of musicology and an index are included.

520. Biancolli, Louis, and Peyser, Herbert F. *Masters of the Orchestra: From Bach to Prokofieff.* New York: G. P. Putnam's Sons, 1954.

Biographies of 14 major Western composers. In addition to a biographical essay, each chapter-length sketch includes descriptions and criticism of the composer's major works.

521. Cross, Milton, and Ewen, David. *The Milton Cross New Encyclopedia of the Great Composers and Their Music.* 2 volumes. Garden City, NY: Doubleday, 1969.

In addition to providing chapter-length biographies of 67 Western composers, the *Milton Cross Encyclopedia* provides a history of Western music before Bach, after Bach, a basic discography, and a description of the symphony orchestra. A dictionary of musical forms and a glossary of basic terms complete this reference work, which is thoroughly indexed and provides bibliographies on each composer.

522. Rosenberg, Deena, and Rosenberg, Bernard. *The Music Makers.* New York: Columbia University Press, 1979.
> Features interviews with contemporary composers, conductors, performers, teachers, managers, patrons, and critics of music in America. Most offer thoughts on their work and the nature of musical performance. A photograph of the subject accompanies each interview, and an index provides access to names.

523. Gelatt, Roland. *Music Makers: Some Outstanding Musical Performers of Our Day.* New York: Alfred A. Knopf, 1953. Reprint. New York: Da Capo Press, 1972.
> This book of essays profiles conductors, singers, string players, keyboardists, a clarinetist, and a guitarist who were prominent influences in classical performance in the early 50s. Most are still alive and well-known today. The biographies are career-oriented and draw heavily from the artist's own words about his/her own work. An insert of portraits is included, as is an index to names and compositions.

524. Ewen, David. *Musicians Since 1900: Performers in Concert and Opera.* New York: H. W. Wilson, 1978.
> Biographical essays accompanied by photographs describe the lives and careers of musicians in this century. At the end is a list of musicians, classified by instrument, voice, or type of performance.

525. Pratt, Waldo Selden. *The New Encyclopedia of Music and Musicians.* New York: Macmillan, 1924.
> This encyclopedia is divided into 3 parts. Part 1 is a dictionary of musical terms, styles and concepts, followed by a bibliographic essay. Part 2 contains biographies of musicians since 1700; an appendix provides information on musicians through the seventeenth century. This portion is interspersed with occasional portraits. Part 3 lists places, institutions, and organizations of interest to musical history, and cites the significance of each.

526. Matz, Mary Jane. *Opera Stars in the Sun: Intimate Glimpses of Metropolitan Personalities.* New York: Farrar, Straus, and Cudahy, 1955. Reprint. Westport, CT: Greenwood Press, 1973.
> Short, gossipy biographical sketches of opera luminaries. Mostly drawn from interviews, the performers' own words make up the body of each profile and are followed by factual vital data, education and training background, and a list of the person's roles at the Metropolitan Opera in New York City. The profiles are divided into 6 chapters and appear alphabetically within them. The only index is a culinary one, providing access to the singers' mention of foods!

527. Clayton, Ellen Creathorne. *Queens of Song: Being Memoirs of Some of the Most Celebrated Female Vocalists Who Have Performed on the Lyric Stage from the Earliest Days of Opera to the Present Time.* Freeport, NY: Books for Libraries Press, 1972.
> Originally published in 1865, this book traces the careers of opera's prima donnas from the first female performers to the mid-nineteenth

century. Subjects were selected for their musical as well as their moral reputations; ladies who let fame go to their heads were excluded.

Following the biographies (which are in chapter form), is a chronological list of operas and their composers, and an "Alphabetical List of Dramatic Composers Not Pre-eminent as Operatic Writers." An index of names and works follows.

528. *Rock Encyclopedia.* See *Lillian Roxon's Rock Encyclopedia* (515).

529. Malone, Bill C., and McCulloh, Judith. *Stars of Country Music: Uncle Dave Macon to Johnny Rodriguez.* Urbana, IL: University of Illinois Press, 1975.

More than 20 stars' careers are profiled in some detail with others mentioned as parts of general chapters or in passing. The relationship of country music to rock and roll and its development in different parts of the country is also explored.

530. Busnar, Gene. *Superstars of Rock: Their Lives and Their Music.* New York: J. Messner, 1980.

Short biographical sketches on 8 individual rock stars (Elvis Presley, Eric Clapton, Jimi Hendrix, Aretha Franklin, Janis Joplin, Donna Summer, Stevie Wonder, and Elton John) and the members of 3 groups (The Beatles, Rolling Stones, and Bee Gees). A bibliography and index are included.

531. Breslin, Herbert H. *The Tenors.* New York: Macmillan, 1974.

Chapter-length biographies of 5 tenors: Richard Tucker, Jon Vickers, Franco Corelli, Placido Domingo, and Luciano Pavorotti. Each chapter is written by a different individual. An index to names and musical works appears at the back of the book.

532. Borland, Carol. *Who's Who in American Music: Classical.* New York: R. R. Bowker, 1983.

Included are biographies of 6,800 active members of the music community. The majority of inclusions are Americans. The publisher plans to update the directory every 2 years (volume 2 published in 1985).

533. Kingsbury, Kenn. *Who's Who in Country and Western Music.* Culver City, CA: Black Stallion Country Press, 1981.

Presents short biographical sketches of 220 country-and-western artists who are established money-makers. Biographies are divided into sections: artists/entertainers; musicians; song writers/music publishers; and record producers and radio personalities. Other sections list the top 10 country songs annually from 1949–79, country-and-western radio stations by city, organizations, awards, and more. The index to names appears at the front of the book. Each entry includes a photograph, and other full-page photos appear throughout the book.

534. Rich, Maria. *Who's Who in Opera: An International Biographical Directory of Singers, Conductors, Directors, Designers, and Administrators. Also Including Profiles of 101 Opera Companies.* New York: Arno Press, 1976.

The subtitle of this book serves as its scope note. Entries include a brief biographical sketch, followed by a list of productions with which the person was affiliated.

535. Bane, Michael. *Who's Who in Rock.* New York: Facts on File, 1981.

> Listed here are 1,200 solo and group performers with a history, notable works, and an evaluation included. There is also an index of songs, real names for performers, and one indexing individual band members.

536. York, William. *Who's Who in Rock Music: The Facts About Every Rock Group, Soloist, Band Member, and Session Player on Record—Over 12,000 Entries.* New York: Scribner, 1982.

> The self-explanatory title of this work indicates its coverage. Entries are brief and purely factual; no criticism or gossip is included.

537. Chilton, John. *Who's Who of Jazz: Storyville to Swing Street.* Philadelphia, PA: Chilton Book Co., 1972.

> A biographical dictionary of American jazz musicians up to 1920. Biographies of 1,000 jazz musicians born before 1920 are included in concise entries.

538. Ewen, David. *The World of Great Composers.* Englewood, NJ: Prentice-Hall, 1962.

> Thirty-seven composers from the sixteenth to twentieth centuries are profiled in narrative form and discussed by the well-known critic. Appendices list principal works and a bibliography.

STAGE AND FILM

539. Highfill, Philip H., Jr.; Burnim, Kalman A.; and Langhans, Edward A. *Biographical Dictionary of Actors, Actresses, Musicians, Dancers, Managers, and Other Stage Personnel in London, 1660–1800.* 10 volumes to date. Carbondale, IL: Southern Illinois University Press, 1973–.

> Completed through Thomas Keyse's profile in 1982's eighth volume, this work is just what its title indicates. Sketches are brief but contain remarkably detailed information. Illustrations appear throughout each volume and include portraits, promptbooks, stage designs, etc.

540. Cohen-Stratyner, Barbara Naomi. *Biographical Dictionary of Dance.* New York: Schirmer Books/Macmillan, 1982.

> Close to 3,000 individuals who were either dance performers or otherwise involved in the development of dance are profiled in this work, which covers European and American figures. Coverage is from the origin of dance in Europe to the contemporary period. The entries include the usual biographical data as well as information on the development of the individual's career. Some entries include listings of works with which the individual was involved and bibliographies.

541. Thomson, David. *Biographical Dictionary of Film.* Rev. ed. New York: William Morrow, 1981.

> Author Thomson describes this massive yet selective dictionary as his "Personal, Opinionated and Obsessive Biographical Dictionary of the Cinema." His work *is* unique in that his criticism of film and acting

pervades each entry, so that even though the standard biographical dictionary form is maintained, the sketches have much more personality than those in other biographical works. Directors and producers are included with the acting professionals. Sketches appear alphabetically and include the subject's real name as well as his/her film name. Years of birth and death, as well as the place of birth, are given. In addition to his critical comments, Thomson offers a list of screen credits, the year of appearance, and cross-references to others involved in the production.

Indices by film title and given name would have been good additions, however, at 682 pages, Thomson has provided enough information to keep most cinema fans satisfied.

542. Rigdon, Walter. *Biographical Encyclopaedia and Who's Who of the American Theatre.* New York: James H. Heineman, 1966.
In addition to biographies of theater people, this book profiles theater groups and theater buildings. There are also lists of New York productions, reprints of playbills from 1959–65, and a list of American plays premiered abroad. The biographical sketches are similar to those found in most "Who's Who"-type works. Theater, film, and television credits are listed separately below the personal data.

543. Pickard, Roy. *A Companion to the Movies: From 1903 to the Present Day.* London: Butterworth Press, 1972.
This directory of cinema in the English-speaking world arranges the films treated by subject category. Following each subject collection is a corresponding "Who's Who" presenting brief biographical sketches of principle actors; from the title page: "A Guide to the leading players, directors, screenwriters, composers, cameramen and other artists who have worked in the English-speaking cinema over the last seventy years." The work includes "over 1,000 entries, including reviews of nearly 100 classic films." In addition, there are extensive appendices listing camera personnel, composers, screenplays, and academy awards, plus a "Who's Who" index.

544. O'Donnell, Monica M. *Contemporary Theatre, Film, and Television: A Biographical Guide Featuring Performers, Directors, Writers, Producers, Designers, Managers, Choreographers, Technicians, Composers, Executives, Dancers, and Critics in the United States and Great Britain.* Detroit, MI: Gale Research, 1984.
This first edition of a new reference work contains listings for more than 1,100 people currently active or no longer professionally active but who have made significant contributions. Future volumes will emphasize currently active people and update/revise already published sketches. Entries include personal data, career information, writings, awards, and sidelights on people. Includes a cumulative index containing references to the 17th edition of *Who's Who in the Theatre.*

545. Sadoul, Georges. Translated, edited, and updated by Peter Morris. *Dictionary of Film Makers.* Berkeley, CA: University of California Press, 1972.
Approximately 1,000 contributors to the art of cinema since 1895 are profiled. Included are directors, scriptwriters, cinematographers, art directors, composers, producers, and inventors—but not performers. There

are representatives from 60 countries. Entries include a filmography usually and a critical appraisal of contributions of the individuals.

546. Moses, Montrose F. *Famous Actor-Families in America.* New York: Thomas Y. Crowell, 1906. Reprint. New York: Greenwood Press, 1968.

This heavily illustrated book provides family histories and genealogies of some of the turn-of-the-century's best-known stage families. Included are families such as the Booths, the Sotherns, the Drews, the Barrymores, and the Powers, among others. The chapters have no distinct scheme or arrangement. A chapter-by-chapter bibliography at the end of the book could prove quite useful to theater history buffs.

547. Young, William C. *Famous Actors and Actresses on the America Stage: Documents of American Theater History.* 2 volumes. New York: R. R. Bowker, 1975.

Over 200 performers have been included in this work, with preference going to eighteenth- and nineteenth-century performers. Twentieth-century performers were also included but only in a representative way. Since eighteenth- and nineteenth-century performers are harder to locate data on, they earned preferential coverage. This illustrated work includes basic biographical data, important roles played, and some narrative on the individuals, including excerpts from reviews. A helpful selective bibliography is provided as well as other finding aids, such as an index by decades and an index to both volumes.

548. Kobbe, Gustav. *Famous Actors and Their Homes.* Boston: Little, Brown, 1905.

Offers gossipy sketches about 7 famous stage actors, emphasizing their home and family life. Heavily illustrated with photographs.

549. ———. *Famous Actresses and Their Homes.* Boston: Little, Brown, 1905.

Offers sketches about several famous turn-of-the-century actresses, with emphasis placed on their home and family lives.

550. Strang, Lewis C. *Famous Actresses of the Day in America. Famous Actors of the Day in America.* 2 volumes. Boston: L. C. Page and Co., 1899–1900.

Chapter-length biographical sketches of late nineteenth-century actresses and actors comprise the text of these twin volumes. In addition to providing biographical data, the author has included his own critical interpretations of their work. Some portraits are included, and an extensive index of names and play titles completes each volume.

551. Stewart, John. *Filmarama.* 2 volumes. Metuchen, NJ: Scarecrow, 1975–.

Filmarama's first 2 volumes, *The Formidable Years, 1893–1919* and *The Flaming Years, 1920–1929*, are the initial installments in what is supposed to become a 6-volume work, with each volume covering a decade in film. Entries are limited to actors and major directors.

The information provided by *Filmarama* is very specific. It includes each subject's life dates, a list of film and stage appearances (limited to New York unless noted otherwise), and the dates of these appearances.

Compiler Stewart indicates the role played in each appearance and if the character was featured in serial films. Each list of works is arranged alphabetically and is divided by type; thus D. W. Griffith's works as an actor precede the films he directed. The index to *Filmarama* is alphabetical by movie title. Next to titles are the date of release and the production company. Numbers follow, which correspond to the numbered entries, thus providing access to a film's entire cast.

552. Miller, Lee O. *Great Cowboy Stars of Movies and Television.* Westport, CT: Arlington House, 1979.

A tribute to the men who helped develop the B-Western film genre. Divided into 3 parts, biographies are of "living legends," those who achieved fame in film or TV between 1950-79, and deceased actors. Sketches include several portraits, quotations from interviews, and a list of Western film credits. There is an index of names and film titles. More than 75 stars are profiled.

553. Maltin, Leonard. *The Great Movie Comedians: From Charlie Chaplin to Woody Allen.* New York: Crown, 1978.

Twenty-two short chapters on movie comedians and comedy teams make up this book. Arranged chronologically, all are actors who gained fame on the American screen. Photographs pepper the text, which is critical as well as biographical. Each sketch concludes with a filmography; there is an index in the back of the book.

554. Blum, Daniel. *Great Stars of the American Stage: A Pictorial Record.* New York: Grosset and Dunlap, 1954.

A photographic biographical dictionary of film stars from the early silents to the 50s. Each subject has 2 pages of coverage, comprised mainly of photographs, ranging from childhood to contemporary portraits. The sketches are one paragraph in length and are arranged in loosely chronological order. The last several sketches are of actors and actresses whom compiler Blum expected to become great; his prophecies were about 50 percent correct. An index by name provides access to the sketches.

555. Wlaschin, Ken. *Illustrated Encyclopedia of the World's Great Movie Stars and Their Films.* New York: Harmony, 1979.

Divided into 3 sections: The Silent Movie Stars; the Classic Movie Stars; and the Modern Movie Stars. This work is international in scope and narrative in style. It lists films made by 400 stars from 1900–79.

556. Gertner, Richard. *International Motion Picture Almanac 1984.* 55th ed. New York: Quigley Publishing, 1984.

Brief biographical data of performers and others affiliated with motion pictures are included along with lists of their films. This work also contains lists of films made between 1955 and 1982, stars of the films, running lengths, pictures made for TV, organizations, and other services related to the industry.

557. Schickel, Richard. *The Men Who Made the Movies: Interviews with Frank Capra, George Cukor, Howard Hawks, Alfred Hitchcock, Vincent Minnelli, King Vidor, Raoul Walsh, and William A. Wellman.* New York: Atheneum, 1975.

Included in this volume are narrative interviews with these great movie directors, some of whose careers go back to the early days of movies.

558. Schuster, Mel. *Motion Picture Performers: A Bibliography of Magazine and Periodical Articles, 1900–1969.* 1 volume plus first supplement. Metuchen, NJ: Scarecrow Press, 1971.

Primarily a bibliography of articles and other publications about major performers of the period. The main volume includes 2,900 performers, and the supplement adds another 2,600.

559. *Notable Names in the American Theatre.* Clifton, NJ: James T. White, 1976.

This is a 10-year update of the *Biographical Encyclopedia and Who's Who of the American Theatre.* There are 9 sections in this book, with the biographical section bearing the same title as the book. People included are in all types of theatrical pursuits as performers, writers, critics, teachers, etc., and are individuals who have made an important contribution to the theatrical world.

560. Tynan, Kenneth. *Show People: Profiles in Entertainment.* New York: Simon and Schuster, 1979.

Profiles of 5 famous late twentieth-century entertainers: Ralph Richardson, Tom Stoppard, Johnny Carson, Mel Brooks, and Louise Brooks.

561. Schickel, Richard. *The Stars.* New York: Bonanza Books, 1962.

A heavily illustrated history of the Hollywood star system, this book opens with a chapter on the "Prototypes" or first members of the star system, and continues by decade through the 1950s, when the structure of the star system collapsed. Each chapter describes a decade in American film and highlights the major stars of that time. An index to names and movie titles is provided.

562. Shaw, Dale. *Titans of the American Stage: Edwin Forrest, the Booths, the O'Neills.* Philadelphia, PA: The Westminster Press, 1971.

Selected because "they made their mark on theatre history through prodigious work, and in the exercise of true talent," these are investigations into the lives of men who shaped American theater. The book is divided into thirds and is illustrated with pen-and-ink drawings, photographs, reproductions of playbills, etc. A bibliography of theater works and specific citations to each man concludes the work, followed by an index to titles and names.

563. Slide, Anthony. *The Vaudevillians: A Dictionary of Vaudeville Performers.* Westport, CT: Arlington House, 1981.

Many vaudevillians came from families of showpeople as these biographical sketches indicate. Vaudeville's heyday spanned about 120 years and gave birth to some major performers as well as to performance forms such as radio. Individuals and teams are profiled with additional references concluding the entertaining and informative entries.

564. Twomey, Alfred E., and McClure, Arthur F. *The Versatiles: A Study of Supporting Character Actors and Actresses in the American Motion Picture, 1930–1955.* South Brunswick, NJ: A. S. Barnes & Co., 1969.

Short, illustrated biographies of the second-tier film actors. A list of film appearances accompanies each entry.

565. Parker, John. *Who Was Who in the Theatre 1912–1976.* 4 volumes. London: Pitman, 1912-22. Reprint. Detroit, MI: Gale Research, 1978.

A bibliographic note inside each volume of this work states: "The 4100 biographical entries in this work represent the latest sketches on the deceased or inactive individuals included in the original series *Who's Who in the Theatre*. The series, edited by John Parker, was published in 15 editions between 1912 and 1972 by Pitman. Updating through 1976 has been added for death dates."

This is an international compilation of biographical profiles of deceased stage personnel, including actors, producers, managers, directors, playwrights, etc. Sketches emphasize each person's professional development, tracing their progress chronologically.

566. Truitt, Evelyn Mack. *Who Was Who on Screen.* New York: R. R. Bowker, 1974.

More than 6,000 screen personalities who died between 1920 and 1971 are included. Coverage is primarily of American, British, and French personalities. Each entry includes a brief biographical sketch and a complete list of screen credits.

567. Ragan, David. *Who's Who in Hollywood 1900–1976.* New Rochelle, NY: Arlington House, 1976.

Short sketches about American motion picture actors, including living players, deceased players who lived between 1900 and 1974, players who died in 1975 and 1976, "lost" players, and "lost" child players. Biographical data are limited to a short description of the kinds of roles the actor performed and a selected list of screen credits.

568. Herbert, Ian. *Who's Who in the Theatre.* 17th ed. 2 volumes. Detroit, MI: Gale Research, 1981.

Volume 1 contains nearly 2,400 narrative biographies. The sketches contain listings of all theater engagements up to the time of publication. The work is primarily concerned with British and American theater, although some recognition is given Australians and Canadians. Volume 2 contains reproductions of playbills of British and American theater productions, including the name of the theater, the performance dates, the title, and credits.

569. Browne, Walter, and Koch, E. DeRoy. *Who's Who on the Stage: A Dramatic Reference Book and Biographical Dictionary of the Theater.* New York: B. W. Dodge, 1908.

An alphabetical listing of actors, actresses, playwrights, and producers who enjoyed prominence on the early twentieth-century American stage. Entries vary in length from a paragraph to several pages, and photographs or drawn portraits are included whenever possible. All of those profiled were living at the time of publication.

VISUAL ARTS

570. Lipman, Jean, and Armstrong, Tom. *American Folk Painters of Three Centuries*. New York: Hudson Hills Press, Inc., 1980.

Artists included are those deemed the best American folk painters by the editors, or those who left a large body of work. Grouped by the century of their major activity, and alphabetically within that century, the majority are from the eastern United States. American Indian art, for example, is not included. Much of what is included is based on previous publications, with an indication at the beginning of each chapter of what the chapter is based on. The biographical information is in narrative form.

571. Dawdy, Doris Ostrander. *Artists of the American West: A Biographical Dictionary*. (The third volume is subtitled: *Artists Before 1900*.) 3 volumes. Chicago: Swallow Press (3d volume is from Ohio University Press), 1974–85.

The 3 volumes, published over the course of a decade, cover artists active before 1900 and working in the 17 states west of the 95th meridian (The 95th meridian was considered a determining point for where the West began.). Vital statistics are included as well as brief narratives for the artists about whom more information was known. All 3 volumes contain more than 4,000 artists. The preface in each volume gives an interesting account of the data-gathering process. A bibliography concludes each volume.

572. Clement, Clara Erskine, and Hutton, Lawrence. *Artists of the Nineteenth Century and Their Works*. 5th ed. rev. 2 volumes in 1. Boston: Houghton, Mifflin and Co., 1889.

Contains over 2,050 entries of nineteenth-century artists from Great Britain, Europe, and the United States. Artists from all of the visual arts, including commercial illustration, are included. Major works are cited with each name, and selected entries include excerpts from reviews and critiques.

573. Kingston, Jeremy. *Arts and Artists*. New York: Facts on File, 1980.

Seventy artists are the subject of this work. Artists included are prominent in sculpture and painting as well as in performing arts. Biographical information is emphasized, not critiques.

574. Hammelmann, Hanns A. (Edited and completed by T. S. R. Boase.) *Book Illustrators in Eighteenth-Century England*. New Haven, CT: Published for the Paul Mellon Centre for Studies in British Art (London) by Yale University Press, 1975.

Presents brief sketches about the artists who supplied engravings and illustrations to English book publishers in the eighteenth century. Personal data are limited and include educational background and information about the artist's style of illustration. A bibliography of works containing the artists' better-known contributions completes each entry. An index to authors and titles enables readers to ascertain which artist illustrated a particular edition; 45 plates provide a representative sampling of works.

575. Williamson, George C. *Bryan's Dictionary of Painters and Engravers in Five Volumes.* 4th ed., rev. and enl. 5 volumes. London: G. Bell and Sons, 1903–19.
Brief entries on major Western painters, illustrators, and engravers make up the contents of this heavily illustrated 5-volume work.

576. Bjerkoe, Ethel Hall, and Bjerkoe, John Arthur. *The Cabinetmakers of America.* Rev. and corrected. Exton, PA: Schiffer Ltd., 1978.
Brief biographical sketches on influential cabinet furniture makers comprise the bulk of this volume. Sketches focus on each individual's career in furniture design and craftsmanship, eliminating all but the most basic personal data. Photographs and etchings of selected pieces are included, as are a short history of American cabinetmaking, a glossary, bibliography, and list of cabinetmakers by state.

577. Emanuel, Muriel. *Contemporary Artists.* 2d ed. New York: St. Martin's Press, 1983.
International in scope, biographical and critical information is included for 1,000 artists. Dead artists are included if they are still regarded as influential. Entries include a short biography; lists of exhibitions; lists of collections in which the artist is represented; a bibliography of publications by and about the artists; and, on occasion, a short, critical, signed essay. Many lesser-known artists are included.

578. Parry-Crooke, Charlotte. *Contemporary British Artists.* New York: St. Martin's Press, 1979.
The first two-thirds of this book are devoted to portraits of the artists and reproductions of their signatures. The biographical sketches are presented as short chronologies of the artist's life. Photographs of selected works and a short, signed, critical essay complete each profile. Each person's major gallery is listed, and a directory of gallery addresses concludes the book.

579. Mahony, Bertha E., and Whitney, Elinor. *Contemporary Illustrators of Children's Books.* Boston: Bookshop for Boys and Girls, 1930. Reprint. Detroit, MI: Gale Research, 1978.
Biobibliographical entries on 150 illustrators are included in this reprint. Twenty-five more illustrators are included in an appendix. Essays on the topic of illustrating for children's books provide additional information about the craft as it had evolved up to the time of original publication in 1930.

580. Walsh, George; Naylor, Colin; and Held, Michael. *Contemporary Photographers.* New York: St. Martin's Press, 1982.
Contemporary Photographers deals with those who are the best and most prominent of living or recently deceased photographers, as well as those from other generations whose work is considered "contemporary." Diversity within the realm of photography is emphasized: portraits, nudes, scientific and technical photography, graphics, social commentary, abstracts, and architectural works are all represented. The 650 profiles give

personal data and employment background, then list exhibitions, collections, and publications in which the photographer's work has been highlighted. If alive and willing to provide it, the photographer's own statement about his/her work follows, along with a critical sketch about the work by a qualified critic.

581. Murray, Peter, and Murray, Linda. *Dictionary of Art and Artists.* New York: Frederick A. Praeger, 1965.
A profusely illustrated guide to Western art history, this alphabetical guide to artists and art masterpieces includes examples of each person's works. An alphabetical bibliography concludes the book.

582. Waters, Grant M. *Dictionary of British Artists Working, 1900–1950.* Eastbourne, England: Eastbourne Fine Art, 1975.
Included are brief entries on more than 5,500 artists. Irish artists are included as well as foreign or colonial artists who worked in Great Britain during the period.

583. Mallalieu, H. L. *The Dictionary of British Watercolour Artists up to 1920.* 2 volumes. Woodbridge, Suffolk, England: Antique Collectors' Club, 1976.
Included are artists who had produced significant work up to the 1920 cutoff date. Brief biographical data plus a description of the artist's work are included. Volume 1 is comprised of the biographies and an appendix, which includes a listing of the pupils of distinguished painters Henry Bright and Peter De Wint and some painters' family trees. Volume 2 is a collection of plates.

584. Cummings, Paul. *Dictionary of Contemporary American Artists.* 4th ed. New York: St. Martin's Press, 1982.
January 1981 was the termination date for inclusion of data on the 923 artists listed in this work. Inclusion is based on representation in collections, representation in major exhibitions, influence as teachers, and recognition received. Entries emphasize exhibitions, awards, where the artist taught or studied, and commissions.

585. Smith, V. Babington. *Dictionary of Contemporary Artists.* Oxford, England: Clio Press, 1981.
Over 10,000 artists are listed with very sparse biographical information: type of artist; birth date and place, if known; and major exhibitions. There is also a listing by category and country, for example, of ceramicists, glass painters, painters, and sculptors.

586. Archibald, E. H. H. *Dictionary of Sea Painters.* Woodbridge, Suffolk, England: Antique Collectors' Club, 1982.
An international guide to painters known for their maritime works. Both living and deceased artists are included, and examples of the artists' work are listed in the entries.

587. Wood, Christopher. *Dictionary of Victorian Painters.* 2d ed. Woodbridge, Suffolk, England: Antique Collectors' Club, 1978.
Includes, in brief entry form, more than 11,000 artists working during the years 1837–1901; some entries provide bibliographic citation information for further reference.

588. Hamilton, Sinclair. *Early American Book Illustrators and Wood Engravers 1670–1870: A Catalogue of a Collection of American Books Illustrated for the Most Part With Woodcuts and Wood Engravings in the Princeton University Library.* 1 volume plus supplement volume. Princeton, NJ: Princeton University Library, 1958, 1968.

Preceding the description of items, which are grouped by illustrator or engraver, is a very brief written sketch of the artist. Volume 2 is a supplement to the main catalog, which was issued in 1958.

589. Samuels, Peggy, and Samuels, Harold. *The Illustrated Biographical Encyclopedia of Artists of the American West.* Garden City, NY: Doubleday, 1976.

Provides biographical data on 1,700 artists who developed Western subjects. Also includes foreign artists who painted Western scenes.

590. Reed, Walt, and Reed, Roger. *The Illustrator in America 1880–1980: A Century of Illustration.* 2d ed. New York: The Society of Illustrators, 1984.

Biographies of 463 American illustrators are grouped by period in this work. For each illustrator, there is a biography citing principle works, awards, and publications in which works appeared. An example of the artist's work appears with each biography. Nearly half of the illustrations are in color. There is a brief bibliography for further reading.

591. Ward, Martha Eads, and Marquardt, Dorothy A. *Illustrators of Books for Young People.* 2d ed. Metuchen, NJ: Scarecrow Press, 1975.

Approximately 750 brief biographies of illustrators are arranged alphabetically by artist's name. Each biography includes titles and dates of publications in which the artist's work appeared. There is an extensive title index.

592. Miller, Bertha E. Mahony; Latimer, Louise Payson; and Folmsbee, Beulah. *Illustrators of Children's Books 1744–1945.* Boston: The Horn Book, Inc., 1947.

This title covers a variety of information about the illustrators of children's books. Part 2 includes over 350 biographical sketches of illustrators living at the time of publication. There is an extensive bibliography in part 3 which includes separate sections for illustrators and authors. There is an index of artists represented by illustrations and a general index.

593. Havlice, Patricia Pete. *Index to Artistic Biography.* 2 volumes plus supplement volume. Metuchen, NJ: Scarecrow Press, 1973, supp. 1981.

Indexes biographical sources on artists. Coverage is international and includes publications dating from 1926 to 1980.

594. Canaday, John. *Lives of the Painters.* 4 volumes. New York: W. W. Norton & Co., 1969.

Primarily a history of painting from Giotto to Cezanne, this work contains several hundred biographies of famous painters arranged by period. Volume 4 contains an extensive collection of representative paintings plus an index of illustrations arranged by painter and a general index to the set.

595. *Macmillan Biographical Encyclopedia of Photographic Artists and Innovators.* New York: Macmillan, 1983.
    International in coverage, this work includes nineteenth- and twentieth-century figures among the 2000 entries and provides data on many artisans who might otherwise prove elusive to locate. Excellent photographs illustrate this book, and there is a listing of museums and galleries that feature photography exhibits.

596. Opitz, Glenn B. *Mantle Fieldings' Dictionary of American Painters, Sculptors, & Engravers.* Rev. ed. Poughkeepsie, NY: Apollo Book, 1983.
    Concise biographical information is provided on over 10,000 artists.

597. *Who's Who in American Art.* 16th ed. New York: R. R. Bowker, 1984.
    Includes listings of 11,000 active artists in the United States, Canada, and Mexico. The usual biographical data are provided, including information on commissions, style, and artistic medium. Also included are a geographic index and a classification index by specialty.

598. Harris, Ann Sutherland, and Nochlin, Linda. *Women Artists: 1550–1950.* New York: Alfred A. Knopf, 1979.
    This exhibition catalog includes biographical information about the female artists whose work was exhibited at a 1979 show in the Los Angeles County Museum of Art (which also holds the copyright for the work).

XIV. Special Groups

NATIVE AMERICANS

599. Brumble, H. David, III. *An Annotated Bibliography of American Indian and Eskimo Autobiographies.* Lincoln, NE: University of Nebraska Press, 1981.
    While this is simply an annotated bibliography to autobiographical sources, it is also a valuable reference to grant researchers access to additional data about some groups that are biographically elusive. There are 500+ entries, covering the eighteenth to twentieth centuries.

600. Littlefield, Daniel F., Jr., and Parins, James W. *A Biobibliography of Native American Writers, 1772–1924.* Metuchen, NJ: Scarecrow, 1981.
    More than 4,000 writers are included in this biobibliography of Native American writers, who are listed by their names as well as by pen names, or by pseudonym only when that is the sole known name. Some of the writers are known only by pen names. There is a listing of works in English by Native Americans (excluding Canada) and covering the period 1772 to the end of 1924. A separate section provides whatever biographical information, including tribe, is available on the writers. There is an index by tribal affiliation as well as a subject index.

601. Buckland, C. E. *Dictionary of Indian Biography.* New York: Haskell House, 1968.
    Approximately 2,600 persons important to Indian history from about 1750 are included: English and foreign individuals are listed in addition to Indians. A lengthy bibliography is appended.

602. Heuman, William. *Famous American Indians.* New York: Dodd, Mead, 1972.
    Biographies of 9 well-known native American leaders are accompanied by old prints and photographs. [Juvenile]

603. Capps, Benjamin. *The Great Chiefs.* Alexandria, VA: Time-Life Books, 1975.
    A history of Native American tribes during the nineteenth century, emphasizing their most influential leaders and tracing the demise of the tribal nations as White expansionism took place. Several of the more famous chiefs are profiled in detail, including Chief Joseph of the Nez

Perce, Sitting Bull, and others. Profusely illustrated, the book also includes an index and a lengthy bibliography.

604. Dockstader, Frederick J. *Great North American Indians: Profiles in Life and Leadership.* New York: Van Nostrand Reinhold, 1977.

An interesting introduction discusses the scarcity of Indian biographical information and the naming of Indians. Three hundred biographies are in this volume, which is intended to be a general reference work to Native North American—male and female—leaders and major Indian families. Emphasis is on contributions the individuals made and a lengthy bibliography encourages further reading; a tribal listing groups the biographees by tribe. There is also a chronological index of the individuals and an index of names.

605. Klein, Bernard, and Icolari, Daniel. *Reference Encyclopedia of the American Indian.* New York: B. Klein & Co., 1978.

In addition to providing general reference information on Native Americans, the *Reference Encyclopedia* includes in volume 2 a "Who's Who" of living Native Americans "prominent in Indian affairs, business, the arts and professions." Non-Indians concerned with Native American politics, history, or arts are also included. Native Americans are listed under their English names, but tribal names and their tribal affiliations are also supplied.

BLACKS

606. Herdeck, Donald E. *African Authors: A Companion to Black African Writing. Volume 1: 1300–1973.* Washington, DC: Black Orpheus Press, 1973–.

The authors covered are primarily from sub-Saharan Africa. Emphasis is on authors of novels, plays, poems, and short stories, although authors of tales, proverbs, and legends are also included. More than 594 authors are listed. Entries are narrative in style and include the author's dates of birth and death, location, and writing genre. Each entry also lists the writer's works. Critical essays on African literature provide additional information and are included in the appendices. Among the many other appendices are: Authors by Chronological Period; and Authors by Genre; Authors by Country of Origin; Authors by African Language or Languages Employed.

607. Cederholm, Theresa Dickason. *Afro-American Artists: A Bio-Bibliographical Directory.* Boston: Trustees of the Boston Public Library, 1973.

Coverage is from the slave craftsman of the 1700s to the time of publication; many obscure artists are included. For some of the artists, only the barest of data were available; for others, numerous awards received and works are included. For each entry, the source of the information is given, an aid to people interested in further research. Also, there is a lengthy bibliography of sources where data on Afro-American artists can be found.

608. Davis, Thadious M., and Harris, Trudier. *Afro-American Fiction Writers After 1955.* Detroit, MI: Gale Research, 1984.

Forty-nine Afro-American authors active since 1955 are analyzed in entertaining essays that describe the writers' career development, critique their work, and provide bibliographies of their writings. This is volume 33 of the Dictionary of Literary Biography series.

609. Southern, Eileen. *Biographical Dictionary of Afro-American and African Musicians.* Westport, CT: Greenwood Press, 1981.

Covered in this volume are 1,400 musicians born between 1640 and 1940. Each entry includes biographical data as well as bibliographies and discographies.

610. Williams, Ethel. *Biographical Directory of Negro Ministers.* 3d ed. Boston, MA: G. K. Hall, 1975.

A "Who's Who" of Afro-American religious leaders. Only living persons are included.

611. Toppin, Edgar A. *A Biographical History of Blacks in America Since 1528.* New York: David McKay Co., Inc., 1971.

Based on "a series of articles that appeared weekly in the *Christian Science Monitor*, March 6 to June 12, 1969," this is a history of the Afro-American experience from the sixteenth to the mid-twentieth centuries. The first half of the book includes an overview of Black history, with a bibliography of additional readings. The second half of the book contains biographies of living and deceased Afro Americans.

612. Inge, M. Thomas; Duke, Maurice; and Bryer, Jackson R. *Black American Writers: Bibliographical Essays.* 2 volumes. New York: St. Martin's Press, 1978.

Volume 1 covers writers of the eighteenth century, slave narratives, early modern writers, the Harlem Renaissance, and Langston Hughes. Volume 2 covers 4 major twentieth-century writers: Richard Wright, Ralph Ellison, James Baldwin, and Amiri Baraka (LeRoi Jones). Essays are bibliographical in nature.

613. Rush, Theressa Gunnels; Myers, Carol Fairbanks; and Arata, Esther Spring. *Black American Writers Past and Present: A Biographical and Bibliographical Dictionary.* 2 volumes. Metuchen, NJ: Scarecrow Press, 1975.

Sketches on over 2,000 Black writers who live/publish in the United States and those deceased individuals who also fit those criteria. Entries provide standard "Who's Who"-type data, in addition to a bibliography of each writer's works, arranged by type. Photographic portraits accompany most entries. Volume 2 includes a general bibliography on Black writers, as well as 2 separate lists of critics, historians, and editors.

614. Matthews, Geraldine O., and the African-American Materials Project Staff. *Black American Writers 1773–1949: A Bibliography and Union List.* Boston: G. K. Hall, 1975.

The African-American Materials Project was an attempt to identify and locate theses, newspapers, periodicals, bibliographies, guides, and pre-1950 imprints concerning the Black experience in America. This work is confined to Black authors writing on the Black experience and includes

1,600 authors of monographs. Arrangement is by subject, with the bibliographic citation and locations provided when known. Dates of authors are also included. The institutions coordinating and supporting this project were Fisk University, North Carolina Central University, Atlanta University, South Carolina State College, Tuskegee Institute, and Hampton Institute.

615. Brignano, Russell C. *Black Americans in Autobiography: An Annotated Bibliography of Autobiographies and Autobiographical Books Written Since the Civil War.* Rev. and expanded ed. Durham, NC: Duke University Press, 1984.

While the entries are concise, the real value of the work may rest with the 5 indexes that provide multiple access points to the included publications: references to the works through activities, professions, occupations; locations and institutions; first publication years; titles; and organizations. This bibliography provides valuable assistance in determining works that may otherwise be unknown.

616. Christopher, Maurine. *Black Americans in Congress.* Rev. and expanded ed. New York: Thomas Y. Crowell Co., 1976.

Originally published in 1971 under the title *America's Black Congressmen, Black Americans in Congress* provides biographical information about the Black men and women elected to serve in the United States Congress from 1870 to 1975. Arranged chronologically, the chapter-length essays are readable accounts of each person's childhood and the events that led to his/her election to Congress.

617. Davis, Lenwood G., and Sims, Janet L. *Black Artists in the United States: An Annotated Bibliography of Books, Articles, and Dissertations on Black Artists, 1779–1979.* Westport, CT: Greenwood Press, 1980.

There are 476 annotated entries plus an index to authors and subjects.

618. Fax, Elton. *Black Artists of the New Generation.* New York: Dodd, Mead & Co., 1977.

An extension of the author's *Seventeen Black Artists* (New York: Dodd, Mead, 1971), this work profiles 20 Black artists whose work developed in the 1950s and 60s. Sketches trace each person's artistic and philosophical development and include quotations from interviews with the author. Photographs of each artist and a representative work appear in a black-and-white insert.

619. Baker, David N.; Belt, Lida M.; and Hudson, Herman C. *The Black Composer Speaks.* Metuchen, NJ: Scarecrow Press, 1978.

Interviews with 15 contemporary Black composers. Each interview is preceded by a short sketch including vital data, educational background, honors, awards, and a short list of works. A checklist of compositions and a bibliography complete each profile. Appendices include a list of music publishers' addresses, recording companies' addresses, and compositions classified by type (e.g., ballet, chamber music, chorus). There is an alphabetical index of names and compositions.

620. McFarlin, Annjennette Sophie. *Black Congressional Reconstruction Orators and Their Orations, 1869–1879.* Metuchen, NJ: Scarecrow Press, 1976.
Contains biographical information about the 16 Black men who served in the United States Congress during Radical Reconstruction, as well as the texts of speeches they made while in office. Bibliographies at the end of each entry provide access to further readings, and portraits accompany some entries.

621. Joint Center for Political Studies. *Black Elected Officials: A National Roster: 1984.* 13th ed. New York: Unipub, 1984.
A state-by-state directory of Blacks holding elective office. Each state's listing opens with demographic information about population; state, federal, county, and municipal governmental structure; the judiciary and law enforcement; and education in that state.

622. Rivelli, Pauline, and Levin, Robert. *Black Giants.* New York: World Publishing, 1970.
Biographical essays/interviews reprinted from *Jazz and Pop* magazine. Most are about controversial or avant-garde jazz artists of the mid- to late-60s.

623. Franklin, John Hope, and Meier, August. *Black Leaders of the Twentieth Century.* Urbana, IL: University of Illinois Press, 1982.
Fifteen prominent Black leaders are covered in biographical essays.

624. Newell, Virginia K., et al. *Black Mathematicians and Their Works.* Ardmore, PA: Dorrance and Co., 1980.
Predominantly a collection of research articles by Black mathematicians, also included are brief sketches about Afro-American mathematicians. Sketches include educational and career data, as well as a list of publications.

625. Katz, William Loren. *Black People Who Made the Old West.* New York: Thomas Y. Crowell, 1977.
Explorers, fur traders, settlers, gold miners, cowpunchers, soldiers, and law enforcement officers are among the Black men and women profiled in this illustrated biographical work. A bibliography and index are included.

626. Haber, Louis. *Black Pioneers of Science and Invention.* New York: Harcourt, Brace & World, Inc., 1970.
Chapter-length biographies of 14 Afro-American scientists and inventors. A bibliography of further readings, illustrations, and an index are included.

627. D'Emilio, John. *The Civil Rights Struggle: Leaders in Profile.* New York: Facts on File, 1979.
Alphabetically arranged sketches on American civil rights movement leaders since 1945. The preface states that: "Men and women who may have had an important impact on the movement but whose careers were focused elsewhere are not included. Thus no Presidents are profiled; nor are...senators...." An introductory essay provides a brief history of the

American civil rights struggle, and a lengthy bibliography offers a list of additional sources.

628. Logan, Rayford W., and Winston, Michael R. *Dictionary of American Negro Biography.* New York: W. W. Norton, 1982.
An annotated bibliography is included in each of the 700 entries, as well as biographical information.

629. Mapp, Edward. *A Directory of Blacks in the Performing Arts.* Metuchen, NJ: Scarecrow Press, 1978.
A directory of living and deceased Afro-American performers. Entries list their life dates, education, special interests, address, honors, career data, performance highlights, films, and compositions.

630. Abdul, Raoul. *Famous Black Entertainers of Today.* New York: Dodd, Mead, 1974.
"Portraits of eighteen representative black entertainers in the fields of concert music, opera, dance, radio, television, recordings, films, and theatre." [Juvenile]

631. Eichholz, Alice, and Rose, James M. *Free Black Heads of Households in the New York State Federal Census, 1790–1830.* Detroit, MI: Gale Research, 1981.
An index to these censuses for this group.

632. Richardson, Ben, and Fahey, William A. *Great Black Americans.* 2d rev. ed. New York: Thomas Y. Crowell, 1976.
Formerly titled *Great American Negroes*, this source is divided into 7 sections, including music, theater, art, literature, education and public affairs, science, and sports. Several representative Afro Americans are selected for each category and are profiled in sketches aimed at a juvenile audience. Thirty-one individuals appear in the book. [Juvenile]

633. Adams, Russell L. *Great Negroes, Past and Present.* 3d ed. Chicago: Afro-Am Publishing, Co., Inc., 1969.
Divided into 12 sections, this reference work offers biographical sketches of Blacks throughout history, from ancient Africa to twentieth-century Americans.

634. Bontemps, Arna. *Great Slave Narratives.* Boston: Beacon Press, 1969.
Three slave memoirs describing life in America's "Peculiar Institution." They are titled: (1) *The Life of Olaudah Equiano, or Gustavus Vassa, the African, Written by Himself;* (2) *The Fugitive Blacksmith; or Events in the History of James C. Pennington, Pastor of a Presbyterian Church, New York, Formerly a Slave in the State of Maryland;* and (3) *Running a Thousand Miles for Freedom; or, The Escape of William and Ellen Craft from Slavery.*

635. Spradling, Mary Mace. *In Black and White: A Guide to Magazine Articles, Newspaper Articles, and Books concerning More than 15,000 Black Individuals and Groups.* 3d ed. 2 volumes plus supplement volume. Detroit, MI: Gale Research, 1980.

Approximately 15,000 groups and individuals are listed in this international guide to sources of information on Blacks in magazine and newspaper articles and in 450 books. There is also an occupation index.

636. Shockley, Ann Allen, and Chandler, Sue P. *Living Black American Authors: A Biographical Directory.* New York: R. R. Bowker, 1973.
Basic information is provided about Black writers in many fields; their publications are also listed. For some, biographical data are not available, but publications are still cited. A list of Black publishers is included, and there is a title index to the works cited.

637. Young, Henry J. *Major Black Religious Leaders Since 1940.* Nashville, TN: Abingdon Press, 1979.
Fourteen leaders are profiled. The importance of the role of religious leaders in civil rights activities becomes clear as one reads the profiles.

638. Popkin, Michael. *Modern Black Writers.* New York: Frederick Ungar Publishing Co., 1978.
Black writers from throughout the world are included in this volume, which is similar in arrangement to *Contemporary Literary Criticism.* Arranged alphabetically by authors' names, each segment includes excerpts of criticism written about the individuals' work. Biographical detail varies, depending on the amount of information supplied by the critic.

639. Burt, Olive W. *Negroes of the Early West.* New York: Messner, 1969.
A work offering brief illustrated biographies of Afro Americans who helped develop the American West. [Juvenile]

640. Dobler, Lavinia, and Toppin, Edgar A. *Pioneers and Patriots: The Lives of Six Negroes of the Revolutionary Era.* Garden City, NY: Doubleday, 1965.
Aimed at children, this book contains illustrated biographies of Benjamin Banneker, Paul Cuffe, John Chavis, Phillis Wheatley, Peter Salem, and Jean Baptiste Pointe de Sable. [Juvenile]

641. Chalk, Ocania. *Pioneers of Black Sport: The Early Days of the Black Professional Athlete in Baseball, Basketball, Boxing, and Football.* New York: Dodd, Mead, 1975.
Divided into 4 sections (one on each sport), this book explores the Black experience in American sports. Biographical information on Black athletes appears throughout the text, and access to the biographies is gained through the index. This volume is unique in that it emphasizes social and historical trends more than the sheer athletic prowess of its subjects.

642. Chittenden, Elizabeth F. *Profiles in Black and White: Stories of Men and Women Who Fought Against Slavery.* New York: Scribner's, 1973.
Short sketches on 12 nineteenth-century Americans who fought the "peculiar institution." Aimed at young readers, most chapters have portraits and illustrations. There is a short bibliography and an index. [Juvenile]

643. Page, James A. *Selected Black American Authors: An Illustrated Bio-Bibliography.* Boston: G. K. Hall, 1977.

Biobibliographies of living and deceased Afro-American writers, novelists, and poets are accompanied by historians, journalists, critics, and librarians who are published authors. Entries include each person's personal data, career and professional background, and a list of publications. Arranged alphabetically, most entries include portraits. Indices to titles and subjects expand the versatility of the book, and a lengthy bibliography of sources completes it.

644. Matney, William C. *Who's Who among Black Americans 1980–81.* 3d ed. Northbrook, IL: Who's Who among Black Americans, 1980.

A "Who's Who" of contributing Afro Americans, this volume contains 13,500 entries and includes cross-indices by geographical location and occupation.

645. Mather, Frank Lincoln. *Who's Who of the Colored Race: A General Biographical Dictionary of Men and Women of African Descent.* Chicago: n.p., 1915. Reprint. Detroit, MI: Gale Research, 1976.

Initial pages give statistics and other information of the 1915 period of the original edition, including population statistics by region, a map showing percentage of Negroes in each state, and miscellaneous data on schools, marital status, and the Emancipation Proclamation. An addendum lists entries received too late for inclusion in the main body of the work. The entries themselves are brief, factual in style, and provide the usual biographical information and list of accomplishments. A large percentage of the entrants are from the field of education or members of the clergy.

646. Rogers, J.A. *World's Great Men of Color.* Rev. ed. 2 volumes. New York: Macmillan, 1972.

Biographies of people throughout the world who trace their origins to Africa. Arranged geographically, then chronologically, the book opens with leaders of antiquity, and ends in twentieth-century America. Each of the 200 sketches includes a bibliography; many contain portraits. A section entitled "Great Men of Color in Brief" provides additional brief sketches.

CHICANOS

647. Martinez, Julio A. *Chicano Scholars and Writers: A Bio-Bibliographical Directory.* Metuchen, NJ: Scarecrow Press, 1979.

Five hundred Chicanos and Anglo-American and Latin American scholars are included in alphabetical arrangement with biographical data, listings of publications, and critiques of their works. Also included is a subject index.

JEWS

648. Lakeville Press. *American Jewish Biographies.* New York: Facts on File, 1982.

Some bibliographical references are included in addition to the biographical information on these 400 prominent Jewish men and women of achievement. A subject index provides access by occupation.

649. Schneiderman, Harry; Karpman, I.J. Carmin; and Karpman, Esther G. *Who's Who in World Jewry: A Biographical Dictionary of Outstanding Jews.* 2d ed. New York: Who's Who in World Jewry, Inc.; distributed by David McKay Co., Inc., 1965.

Contains approximately 11,000 biographies of Jews from throughout the world, although almost half are from the United States. Automatically admitted were high government officials and academicians holding the rank of assistant professor or higher.

WOMEN

650. Stineman, Esther. *American Political Women: Contemporary and Historical Profiles.* Littleton, CO: Libraries Unlimited, 1980.

Coverage is of prominent women in politics at the time of compilation and of women formerly in office and who were regarded as worthy of inclusion. Sixty women are profiled with biographical data plus citations of sources for additional information. Much of the information was gleaned from the author's interviews with the individuals, so the usual biographical information is supplemented by information on preparation for political office and viewpoints on issues of the day. There is also an extensive bibliography as well as appended lists of women who served in specific types of political offices.

651. Willard, Frances E., and Livermore, Mary A. *American Women: Fifteen Hundred Biographies with over 1,400 Portraits.* Rev. ed. 2 volumes. New York: Mast, Crowell, and Kirkpatrick, 1893. Reprint. Detroit, MI: Gale Research, 1973. (See also *A Woman of the Century: Fourteen Hundred-Seventy Biographical Sketches Accompanied by Portraits of Leading American Women in all Walks of Life.*)

A second subtitle to this work describes its scope: "A Comprehensive Encyclopedia of the Lives and Achievements of American Women During the Nineteenth Century." A classified index at the end of volume 2 assigns each woman profiled a professional designation, ranging from actors and archaeologists to telegraph operators, temperance workers, and even a wood-carver. Information about family background, offspring, and husbands is also included.

652. Tick, Judith. *American Women Composers Before 1870.* Ann Arbor, MI: UMI Research Press, 1983.

This book is devoted mainly to an overall study of female musical composition in the United States prior to 1870. However, chapter 7, entitled, "Five Mid-Nineteenth Century Composers," explores the lives, education, and development of 5 women whose compositions were published and saw a degree of recognition. An appendix provides a checklist of "Selected Compositions Published by Women in the U.S. before 1870," and the index refers readers to information about other female composers in the text.

653. Howes, Durwood. *American Women, 1935–40: A Composite Biographical Dictionary: A Consolidation of All Material Appearing in the 1939–1940 Edition of American Women, with a Supplement of Unduplicated Biographical Entries from the 1935–1937 and 1937–1938 Editions.* 2 volumes. Detroit, MI: Gale Research, 1981.
> The title of this work describes the source of the information it contains. The result is a listing of 12,000 women with the usual concise biographical data provided. There are also geographical and occupational indices, an index of women's organizations, and a statistical summary.

654. Duke, Maurice; Bryer, Jackson R.; and Inge, M. Thomas. *American Women Writers: Bibliographical Essays.* Westport, CT: Greenwood Press, 1983.
> Twenty-four major women authors are covered in essays which include information on the authors' works and a critique of their style and contributions.

655. Mainiero, Lina. *American Women Writers: A Critical Reference Guide from Colonial Times to the Present.* 4 volumes. New York: Frederick Ungar Publishing Co., 1979–82.
> Only very well-known or controversial women writers have been widely included in texts for many years; this volume attempts to include information on many more women. Each volume lists the writers included in the total 4-volume set. Each essay is prefaced by the life dates of the writer, parentage, and husband. The essays are descriptive and critical and include lists of writers' works and sources of additional information. In each essay, the biographee is referred to by initial only. Volume 4 includes an index to the entire set.

656. Cameron, Mabel Ward, and Lee, Erma Conkling. *The Biographical Cyclopaedia of American Women.* 2 volumes. New York: Halvord and Franklin W. Lee Publishing Companies, 1924–25. Reprint. Detroit, MI: Gale Research, 1974.
> Approximately 200 biographies are included in volume 1. Selection includes women in the arts and professions and even mothers of famous offspring. Biographies are arranged in random order, so the index is necessary to locate individual biographies.

657. Green, Mildred Denby. *Black Women Composers: A Genesis.* Boston: Twayne Publishers, 1983.
> Explores the works of 5 Black women who have blended "jazz, blues, and spiritual elements and the traditions of Western European music." Each chapter offers a brief overview of the subject's life, education, and career, then examines her compositions in terms of tradition, style, and form. Portraits accompany each sketch. A bibliography and catalog of

music works enable readers to pursue further study of their work, as does a short discography.

658. Emberlin, Diane. *Contributions of Women: Science.* Minneapolis, MN: Dillon Press, 1977.
Six women are profiled in this book aimed toward juveniles. Nine others are briefly profiled at the end of the book. [Juvenile]

659. Bird, Caroline. *Enterprising Women.* New York: W. W. Norton & Company, 1976.
This book was "A Bicentennial Project of the Business and Professional Women's Foundation." More than 46 women innovators from U.S. history are profiled. Some were craftspeople, others were professionals; some were entrepreneurs, others served as inspiration. The women profiled are discussed in narratives that group them together in general categories.

660. Crawford, Anne, et al. *The Europa Biographical Dictionary of British Women: Over 1000 Notable Women from Britain's Past.* London: Europa Publications, Ltd., 1983.
Profiles female British leaders from the Anglo-Saxon period through the twentieth century. Only deceased persons are included, and they fall into 4 categories: women "who sought to expand women's involvement in public affairs"; "those who played a part in shaping history by virtue of their participation in a movement"; "those who influenced the course of events in a more informal way"; and "those who pursued traditional female occupations."

661. Stoddard, Hope. *Famous American Women.* New York: Thomas Y. Crowell Co., 1970.
Forty-one alphabetically arranged biographies of American women who have affected history, society, or the arts in the United States. The profiles are short chapters and include bibliographic references. An index provides cross- references to other names and concepts.

662. Griswold, Rufus Wilmot. *The Female Poets of America.* Rev. ed. New York: James Miller, Publisher, 1873.
This is a collection of selected verse written by American women from colonial days through the mid-nineteenth century. Most have a brief biocritical sketch preceding the poetry selections. There are some portraits, and an alphabetical index of names provides quick access to each poet's works, which are arranged chronologically.

663. *Foremost Women in Communications: A Biographical Reference Work on Accomplished Women in Broadcasting, Publishing, Advertising, Public Relations, and Allied Professions.* New York: R. R. Bowker, 1970.
Concise biographical data on industry leaders plus geographical and subject cross-indexes.

664. Uglow, Jennifer S. *The International Dictionary of Women's Biography.* New York: Continuum, 1982.
Essays on an international roster of influential women, both living and dead. North Americans, Europeans, and women from the British Com-

monwealth countries dominate the entries, but other regions are represented as well. A classified subject index appears at the end.

665. Cohen, Aaron I. *International Encyclopedia of Women Composers.* New York: R. R. Bowker, 1981.
Biographies of women composers from ancient times to the present are included: 5,000 from 70 countries with complete biographies of 3,700. At the time of publication, two-thirds were still living; one-third were from the United States. Each biography lists basic biographical data followed by a listing of biographee's compositions.

666. Opfell, Olga S. *Lady Laureates: Women Who Have Won the Nobel Prize.* Metuchen, NJ: Scarecrow Press, 1978.
Extensive biographies of 16 women who have won the Nobel Prize. There is a photograph of each biographee. The author includes a listing of important dates and the Nobel-related events many of them represent, a bibliography grouped by Nobel Prize winner, and a subject index.

667. McHenry, Robert. *Liberty's Women.* Springfield, MA: G. & C. Merriam, 1980.
One thousand brief biographical sketches of living and deceased women whom the editor views as significant are included. Some prominent individuals are excluded; the selection criteria are not included.

668. *The Living Female Writers of the South.* Philadelphia, PA: Claxton, Remsen, and Haffelfinger, 1872. Reprint. Detroit, MI: Gale Research, 1978.
The essays on 183 women authors are both biographical and bibliographical in nature. Entries are grouped by state. It is necessary to use the index to locate specific authors or their works. An introductory essay mentions additional writers not included. The climate of the time in which these essays were written—post-Civil War, mid-Reconstruction—is clearly evident.

669. Chamberlin, Hope. *A Minority of Members: Women in the U.S. Congress.* New York: Praeger Publishers, 1973.
Sketches/profiles of women in Congress through the 1972 elections.

670. Gutman, Bill. *Modern Women Superstars.* New York: Dodd, Mead, 1977.
Sports biographies of 6 prominent female athletes, all of whom achieved prominence during the 1970s. All are White; 5 of them are American. Each represents a different sport: tennis, ice skating, gymnastics, equestrian competition, skiing, and golf. Exclusion of track and field events, basketball, and volleyball eliminated many minority women. The entries emphasize each woman's development, training, and achievements in her chosen area of competition.

671. The American Mothers Committee, Inc. Bi-Centennial Project, 1974–1976. *Mothers of Achievement in American History, 1776–1976.* Rutland, VT: Charles E. Tuttle, 1976.
This work contains 520 biographical sketches, grouped by state.

672. Sicherman, Barbara, et al. *Notable American Women: The Modern Period—A Biographical Dictionary.* Cambridge, MA: Belknap Press of Harvard University Press, 1980.

A twentieth-century update of the original 3-volume set, *Notable American Women: The Modern Period,* profiles women who died between January 1, 1951, and December 31, 1975. Its purpose is to bring women's history up to date beyond passage of the nineteenth amendment and into the women's movement of the 1960s. Includes a bibliography of other information sources as well as a classified list of women profiled, arranged by profession.

673. James, Edward T. *Notable American Women 1607–1950: A Biographical Dictionary.* 3 volumes. Cambridge, MA: Belknap Press of Harvard University Press, 1971.

In the late 1960s, a group of editors under the sponsorship of Radcliffe College undertook the task of righting a wrong that had stood unassailed for almost 2 centuries: They began to produce a biographical dictionary of women who had made a contribution to the nation's development but had been ignored by previous compilers because of their sex. Each entry includes a list of sources, including government documents and manuscript collections.

674. Wallace, Irving. *The Nympho and Other Maniacs.* New York: Simon and Schuster, 1971.

Wallace divided this amusing volume into 3 books: "the mistress as a scandal"; "the heroine as a scandal"; and "the rebel as a scandal." Indeed the common thread tying the biographies together is that each woman was involved in some type of disgrace. Thirty women are profiled.

675. Diamondstein, Barbaralee. *Open Secrets: Ninety-Four Women in Touch with Our Time.* New York: Viking Press, 1972.

Politicians, entertainers, artists, writers—all women who have made a mark on this century's events—were asked 56 questions ranging from biographical points to the meaning of "male chauvinism" to the political power of women.

676. Nevin, James B. *Prominent Women of Georgia.* Atlanta, GA: The National Biographical Publisher, n.d.

Published in the late 1920s or early 30s, this volume contains portraits and short biographies of women both socially and professionally prominent.

677. Hast, Adele. *Who's Who of American Women.* 14th ed. Chicago: Marquis Who's Who, 1984. Annual.

Included are biographies of 21,000 women in all fields of endeavor.

678. Willard, Frances E., and Livermore, Mary A. *A Woman of the Century: Fourteen Hundred-Seventy Biographical Sketches Accompanied by Portraits of Leading American Women in All Walks of Life.* Buffalo, NY: Charles Wells Moulton, 1893. Reprint. Detroit, MI: Gale Research, 1967. (See also *American Women: Fifteen Hundred Biographies with over 1,400 Portraits.*)

Biographies of American women who had made their mark on society or culture. Both living and deceased women are profiled, and a few non-Americans are included. Some women are listed because of their famous husbands, but many have careers of their own in such diverse fields as medicine, politics, philosophy, and the arts and letters.

679. Leonard, John William. *Woman's Who's Who of America: A Biographical Dictionary of Contemporary Women of the United States and Canada, 1914–1915.* New York: American Commonwealth Company, 1914. Reprint. Detroit, MI: Gale Research, 1976.
Almost 10,000 women living during the years 1914–15 were included in this volume. An effort was made to include women from all walks of life.

680. Bachmann, Donna G., and Piland, Sherry. *Women Artists: An Historical, Contemporary and Feminist Bibliography.* Metuchen, NJ: Scarecrow Press, 1978.
Coverage is of artists born pre-1930. Access is through the table of contents since there is no index. The introduction describes the particular problems faced by women in the art world. The first bibliographical section is of annotations of general works about women artists. Following that is a group of bibliographies of works about more than 150 women artists. Coverage is from the Middle Ages into the twentieth century.

681. Paxton, Annabel. *Women in Congress.* Richmond, VA: Dietz Press, 1945.
Brief profiles of women in Congress, grouped through the 79th Congress.

682. Herman, Kali. *Women in Particular: An Index to American Women.* Phoenix, AZ: Oryx Press, 1984.
This work is an index to more than 15,000 American women from 1500 to the present. The entries are grouped first by "Field and Career" and then chronologically by birth year. Basic biographical data are provided as well as an indication of additional sources. Emphasis is on women of the past rather than those of the present.

683. Center for the American Woman and Politics, Eagleton Institute of Politics, Rutgers—The State University of New Jersey. *Women in Public Office: A Biographical Directory and Statistical Analysis.* 2d ed. Metuchen, NJ: Scarecrow Press, 1978.
From the compilation of the first edition in 1975 to compilation of the second, women in public office increased from 5 to 8 percent. The second edition also includes data on women no longer in office since the 1975 survey and offers an analysis of male and female officeholders. This second edition includes more than 17,000 female public officials at all levels. The statistical analysis—a profile of women in office in 1977—begins the book and is followed by the biographical directory, divided by federal level, and then subdivided by state levels. Data are brief and very basic. Individuals are grouped by office held—mayor, legislator, etc.—not alphabetically. A name index completes the compilation.

684. Raven, Susan, and Weir, Alison. *Women of Achievement: Thirty-Five Centuries of History.* New York: Harmony Books, 1981.
Five hundred women of achievement, primarily from the nineteenth and twentieth centuries, are profiled.

685. Truman, Margaret. *Women of Courage.* New York: William Morrow & Co., 1976.
Profiles of 12 American women who demonstrated courage in their approach to life. Some are famous already, such as Elizabeth Cady Stanton, Susan B. Anthony, and Margaret Chase Smith. Others are less well-known and include Blacks and Native Americans.

686. Laurence, Anya. *Women of Notes: 1000 Women Composers Born Before 1900.* New York: Richards Rosen Press, Inc., 1978.
Offering international coverage, this work provides brief biographical sketches of women who composed/performed classical music. Each entry includes a list of works. An appendix includes a list of other women who contributed to the world of music and a discography of works cited in the sketches.

687. Sabin, Francene. *Women Who Win.* New York: Random House, 1975.
Profiles of 14 female athletes from the United States.

XV. Award Winners

688. Committee on Veterans' Affairs. United State Senate. 96th Congress, First Session, Senate Committee Print Number 3. *Medal of Honor Recipients, 1863–1978*. Washington, DC: U.S. Government Printing Office, 1979.

This volume includes all recipients of the Medal of Honor and is complete through 1976. Included are recipients from all branches of service. Prefatory material includes historical background on the Medal of Honor and illustrations of medals and significant documents. The body of the work consists of brief sketches of medal recipients arranged alphabetically by wars, campaigns, and other military engagements beginning with the Civil War and ending with Vietnam. In addition are separate listings of Medal of Honor recipients arranged by state, a listing of foreign-born recipients, and a comprehensive listing of all Medal of Honor recipients.

689. Walter, Claire. *Winners: The Blue Ribbon Encyclopedia of Awards*. New York: Facts on File, 1978.

Covers 1,000 awards and the 30,000 winners of those awards. Arrangement is by award category with a table of contents for each category. Access is facilitated through the index.

Index

Compiled by Linda Webster

This index includes the authors and titles of biographical sources, as well as subjects. Numbers refer to item numbers in the text.

Ticknor, Caroline, 369
Times, 127
Tishman, Jeffrey, 326
Titans of the American Stage (Shaw), 562
Tobin, James Edward, 254
Toothill, Elizabeth, 283
Toppin, Edgar A., 611, 640
Torrence, Clayton, 89
Townsend, Peter, 231
Trachtenberg, Stanley, 345
Traub, Hamilton, 346
Treasury of Intimate Biographies
    (Snyder), 23
Truitt, Evelyn Mack, 566
Truman, Margaret, 685
Tudor Age, 240
Tunney, Christopher, 143
Tunucci, Barbara A., 310
Turner, Roland, 289
Twentieth-Century American Dramatists
    (MacNicholas), 442
Twentieth-Century American Historians
    (Wilson), 443
Twentieth Century American Nicknames
    (Urdang et al.), 122
*Twentieth-Century American
    Science-Fiction Writers* (Cowart
    and Wymer), 444
*Twentieth-Century Author Biographies
    Master Index* (McNeil), 445
Twentieth Century Authors (Kunitz and
    Haycraft), 446
Twentieth Century Children's Writers
    (Kirkpatrick), 447
*Twentieth-Century Crime and Mystery
    Writers* (Reilly), 448
*Twentieth Century Romance and Gothic
    Writers* (Vinson), 449
Twentieth-Century Science-Fiction Writers
    (Smith), 450
Twentieth Century Western Writers
    (Vinson), 451
Twomey, Alfred E., 564
*Tyler's Quarterly Historical and
    Genealogical Magazine,* 80
Tynan, Kenneth, 560

Uden, Grant, 145
Uglow, Jennifer S., 664
Ujifusa, Grant, 174
Unger, Leonard, 357
Union of Soviet Socialist Republics. *See*
    USSR
Unions. *See* Labor movement
United Kingdom. *See* Great Britain
United Nations, 116

United States biographies. *See*
    Biographies
U.S. Congress. *See* Congress
U.S. Navy Biographical Dictionary
    (Schuon), 168
University faculty, 313, 318, 320
Untermeyer, Louis, 425
Urban, Paul K., 111
Urdang, Laurence, 122
Urdang (Laurence) Associates, 239
USSR, 111, 115

Valentine, Alan, 92
Van Antwerp, Margaret, 409
Van Doren, Charles, 54
Vanderbilt family, 234
Vandiver, Frank E., 65
Vaudevillians (Slide), 563
Versatiles (Twomey and McClure), 564
Vexler, Robert I., 229
Vice-presidential defeated candidates, 222
Vice-presidents, 216, 218, 229
Vice-Presidents and Cabinet Members
    (Vexler), 229
Victorian Novelists After 1885 (Nadel and
    Fredeman), 452
Victorian Novelists Before 1885 (Nadel
    and Fredeman), 453
Victorian Poets After 1850 (Fredeman and
    Nadel), 454
Victorian Poets Before 1850 (Fredeman
    and Nadel), 455
Victorian writers, 452–455
Vidal, Gore, 234
Vincent, Benjamin, 10
Vinson, James, 395, 397, 398, 415, 430,
    434, 449, 451
Violinists, 507
Virginia
    families, 79, 80
    immigrants, 72
    marriage records, 87
    records, 86
    vital records, 88
    wills, 89, 90
Virginia Land Records, 86
*Virginia Magazine of History and
    Biography,* 79
Virginia Marriage Records, 87
Virginia Vital Records, 88
*Virginia Wills and Administrations
    1632–1800* (Torrence), 89
Virginia Wills Records, 90
Visual arts. *See* Artists; Illustrators;
    Painters; Photographers; Sculptors

Wakelyn, Jon L., 65